I0558524

BEAUTIFUL

MOURNING

A Guide to Life After Loss

By

MELISSA OATMAN

To My Family

This book is dedicated to all the people that I have lost in my life, especially to the woman I chose to be my mom. It wasn't until I became a mom myself that I understood how difficult and challenging her job as a mom was. She was my rock, my confidant, my best friend, and my idol. A little part of my world died the day she left this one. There are days when I don't know how I am supposed to make it here without her, but I know she is here guiding my steps. I don't always understand why she had to leave so soon, but I was blessed to have 44 years with her. I only hope to be the best mom to Ally and Christopher. I also dedicate this book to them. They inspire me to keep going each and every single day. I am so proud of who they are becoming, and I hope I make them proud too. I want to thank the amazing women I've been blessed to have in my life who were mom figures to me before and after my mom passed. Lori, Sandy, Grandma Lassen, Aunt Gee, Aunt Connie, you were all so instrumental in shaping who I am today. Thank you so much. To Lori, thank you for always being like a second mom to me. You always give good advice and are willing to listen when I need to vent. To Sandy, growing up next door to you was such a blessing. To Donna and Michele, thank you for taking Mom to her treatments and for the years of many laughs. To my dad and Phil, thank you for all you have done for me throughout the years and when Mom passed. We've had so many laughs and adventures. I will always remember Maine, and Mom loved spending time with Phil in Florida. To Aunt Connie, thank you for taking such good care of Mom in her last stages of life. We are forever grateful to you. You are and will always be the fun aunt. To my sister Mary, we've been best friends since birth. Thank you for always making time for me and for all of our adventures. To my brother Chris, thanks for loving me even though you only wanted one brother. I love you and Mary more than words could express. Dave, David and Ginna, I give a special thanks to you for loving me and being there for me always. To Tori, thank you for providing a place for us to grieve and celebrate my mom. Your kindness and compassion will not soon be forgotten. To my best friend Rusty, who has been instrumental in my writing, thank you for always having my back. I will always love you like butta. I have so many amazing friends and family, and that is what this life is all about. It's not the things that matter. It's the people and the love you share that is truly important. That is all you take with you when you leave this world.

CONTENTS

CHAPTER 1

PAIN LIKE NO OTHER: WHEN GRIEF
FIRST STRIKES

Grief is an interesting thing. Everyone experiences it at some point in their life, yet no two people have the same grief journey. When grief first strikes you, it is shocking, painful, and confusing. Grief is a very complex thing. It is intense. If you've ever been impacted by grief (spoiler alert: everyone has!), it can be downright overwhelming. It feels like you are on the receiving end of a surprise attack by a huge infantry. Only the infantry here is an army of your emotions. They seem to come from every direction and hit you all at the same time. You are confused, lost, hurt, angry, hungry...wait, did she just say hungry? Yes, I did. I'm always hungry. Don't judge me. Anyway, you never really know what emotion will hit you next. It's like a treacherous battlefield where you are attacked from all sides, and you are left wondering what the hell just happened.

Experts often refer to grief as a journey. What an interesting word choice! Why is grief referred to as a journey? When I think about the word journey, a fantastic, fun, and exciting adventure comes to mind. I think of trips to

Europe or beautiful scenic hiking trails. We used to drive eight hours to see my relatives in Michigan. Those trips were always filled with laughter, singing in the car, and 20 stops for food along the way. It was exciting and, yes, food-filled. I'm hungry again, but I digress. Journeys are supposed to be magical and fun. A journey is not what I picture at all when I hear the word grief. Grief is not exciting, it's not a great adventure, and there is absolutely nothing fun about it either. Grief is excruciating and cruel. That is why I like to think of it as an attack. It is relentless, and just when you think you start to feel better, it strikes you again seemingly out of nowhere. Grief just plain sucks, and it changes your whole life. Every person that I have ever talked to about grief said that it changed them in a major way. I lost my mom to cancer in 2022, and it changed me profoundly. This is my story of grief and how it shook me to my very core.

If you were to look up the word *journey* in the dictionary, you would see that the word is defined as "an act of traveling from one place to another." Maybe that is why they call grief a journey. Although you don't physically travel from one place to another, your emotions take you from one place to another every single day. It's like standing on the shore of a beach. One moment, the waves of emotion are small and manageable. Everything is calm, and you think to yourself, "Maybe I can get through the rest of my life without my loved one around. Maybe I will be OK." On other days, the waves are so enormous and torrential that you wonder how you can remain standing.

The waves are so forceful that when they hit you, they knock the breath out of you. The current takes you under, and you can't even seem to keep your head above water. That's what grief is. At least, it is in my own experience. Grief drags you and carries you from one emotion to the next and from one day to the next. One moment, you don't know how you can live even one more second when you are missing your loved one so badly. In other moments, your emotions are calmer and more manageable. Then there are days when your emotions are everywhere in between. You never really know what will set those gigantic waves of grief in motion, and you never know how you will feel each day when you wake up or even from moment to moment. All it takes to change your day is one thought, one memory, or one person asking about your loved one. These experiences can trigger an entire tsunami of emotion in just a matter of seconds.

Grief is such a heavy subject that I try to infuse a little comic relief in my writing; plus, humor has a powerful healing effect, at least it does for me. If you read my previous book (What do you mean you haven't read it yet?), you will know that I'm a very sarcastic person, and my sarcasm brings people so much joy. I bring people a lot of joy merely by being me. Did I mention that I'm also an extremely humble person? Back to the point. It's good to laugh. Laughter is a natural healer. Speaking of laughter, comparing grief to waves in the ocean reminds me of a humorous memory. I love retelling this story because I can still hear my mom's laughter in it. Her laughter was one of the best sounds ever. It was contagious. One summer, a group of my mom's friends and I went to the beach in Gulf Shores. If you've been there, you know how rough the waves can be. One of our friends was fighting the waves trying to walk back to the shore from the ocean. The waves were knocking her all around. She was trying to hold her hat, walk, and avoid being knocked down all at the same time. The view from where we were swimming was quite amusing. We would say, "Oh, she's up. Oh wait, she's down." That continued over and over again for several minutes. She ended up crawling back to the shore. Let's just say she was not thrilled with us, but we couldn't stop laughing. The more we tried to stop laughing, the harder we laughed, and the more angry our friend became. This of course became a vicious cycle. My mom was laughing the hardest. It looked like a scene taken straight out of the I Love Lucy show.

I mention this story not only to make you laugh, but also because it reminds me of the grief journey. When we are living with grief, we're merely trying to move on in our lives. We're just trying to reach the shore from the depths of grief, but we keep getting knocked back down again and again by the tumultuous waves. We're tired, drained, and left crumpled in a ball on the shore. Let me tell you that just as my friend was not thrilled with us for laughing at her, I'm not too thrilled with grief either. Grief makes getting through a regular day all the more difficult. It feels so heavy, unfair, and vindictive.

I have experienced grief many times throughout my life. The strongest and most intense experience of grief for me was when I lost my mom to pancreatic cancer in January of 2022. I was very close to my mom. She was one of my best friends. Not only did we lose her, but we also had to watch her suffer, waste away, and become a shadow of her former self from this horrible disease. It was shocking because she was so full of life before her diagnosis. She was a retired teacher, but she continued to sub.

I used to joke with her that she made retirement look difficult. That was her. Her love for teaching and her students was so intense that she continued to work. Even though she retired, she still wanted to keep teaching. It was her heart and soul. When I'm retired, that's all, folks. I will not be doing much, except maybe traveling. Not her. She adored teaching. It was who she was. Her death is the loss that deeply changed my life, and it is the reason that I am sitting here writing this book today. I have been a completely different person since she passed, and I have been through every emotion there is about a million times. Her loss has made me question everything I thought I knew about life, and my life will never be the same again.

My mom was not my first instance of loss, but hers was the most painful of my life, and believe me, I know firsthand what it is to experience pain. I'm a child of the 80s, after all. I wore Jellies. For the younger crowd, those were plastic shoes. They looked super cute, but those things were excruciating. They rubbed blisters on your toes and on the backs of your heels. People say fashion comes with a price. I guess that price is pain. Speaking of pain, my first experience with loss was when I was 7 years old. My great uncle passed away two days before my eighth birthday. It was a very deep loss for me. He was more than just a great uncle. We lived next door to him and saw him almost every single day. We often spent the night at his house because my great-aunt took care of us for my mom while she worked. He didn't have any grandkids, and both of my grandpas died before I was born. He was, for all intents and purposes, our grandpa. We even called him PaPa. He was the kindest and most joyful person, and his laugh was infectious. He adored us, and we knew it. We had him wrapped around our little fingers. He would do anything for us. There was even a time when he cracked a raw Easter egg on his head. We wanted to trick him, so we told him that it was a hard boiled egg. He knew it wasn't, but he went along with our little prank and cracked it on his head anyway. We giggled, and he smiled and laughed at our delight as the raw egg dripped down his forehead. I didn't learn until many years later that he knew the egg was raw. That's how much he loved making us laugh.

I remember the day he died just like it was yesterday. It will be forever etched in my mind. I had just seen him a day or two before. My eighth birthday was in a few days. He teased me and asked if I wanted a watch for my birthday. He knew that all I wanted was a Cabbage Patch Kid.

I was sitting in my second-grade classroom a few days later, when they called over the intercom to say that I had an early dismissal. I was so happy. I high-fived my friend and raced down to the office. I never got any early dismissals. When I got there, my mom and her friend were waiting. They had very serious expressions on their faces. My mom waited until we got home to tell us the news. "PaPa died this afternoon," she said solemnly. I didn't believe her at first, and I told her to stop lying. She urged me to go next door and see for myself. My sister and I walked next door and the house was full of people. My great-aunt was sitting with her head in her hands, crying. It scared me so much. I remember walking over to her, sitting on her lap, and hugging her. I heard someone say, "Oh, isn't that sweet? She's trying to comfort her." The truth is that I was trying to comfort myself. I was so sad and scared. I was confused and hurt. Everything felt different then. The days that followed were busy and crazy. The family came in from out of town. There was a wake and a funeral, and we had a small gathering to celebrate our birthday in between all of that craziness. There was both laughter and sadness. Thinking back on those memories brings up so much emotion.

I received my first diary for my birthday that year. My very first entry in that diary was about my PaPa dying. It still sends a twinge of pain to my heart to think about that time in my life. There are times when I try to remember what my PaPa's voice sounded like, and I can't. That loss was devastating for me at the time for many reasons. I had never really experienced the death of someone so close before. I didn't understand what was happening, and because I was only 7, I was too young to grasp what death was. It was scary. I couldn't really process what was happening. I didn't know where he went. Everyone kept saying that he went to heaven. I didn't know what going to heaven meant. I just knew he wasn't coming back.

After he passed, they sold his things at auction. That ripped my heart out, and since we lived next door, we had to watch them sell all of his things to the highest bidder. It was as if he never existed. His things were just gone. At least before the auction, if I wanted to be reminded of him, I could just look at his motorcycle in the garage. Now, that was gone too. I was very angry about this, as a 7-year-old little girl who didn't understand why it needed to be done. Even as I am writing this now, it brings me to the present. We also had to sell my mom's belongings. I will never forget the day that we were going through her house; my daughter broke down and started sobbing. It was completely overwhelming for her. She was expressing what we were all feeling. It was as overwhelming to me at 45 as it was to me when I was 7. My PaPa's death was the first death that really shook me to my core, and it made me start to question what happens to us when we die. Will I ever see my PaPa again? Will I ever feel better again? I was so scared of losing anyone else in my family that I remember praying about it the night after I found out he died. I spent the night at my Grandma Lassen's house. She was my mom's mom, and we were very close to her. As I watched her walking around in the kitchen, I worried that God might take her too. I remember praying and asking God not to take my Aunt Gee (my PaPa's wife), my Grandma Lassen, or my mom and dad until I was very old (at least 40). Well, 40 seemed old to a 7-year-old. I now understand that it is not old... I said it's not old! I'm still quite young...in my mind anyway. In what I now think is a very strange coincidence, I would later go on to lose my Aunt Gee in 2019, my grandma in 2020, and my mom in 2022. I wish I could go back and change my prayer now. I was just kidding, God. Please bring them back. 40 years wasn't long enough. I should have said 60. Why did you listen to a stupid kid? And no, I don't truly believe God decided to take them all when I was in my 40s because I prayed for it. I mean, why would God do what a 7-year-old told Him to do? I didn't know anything at that age. All I cared about was whether I was getting a Cabbage Patch doll for my birthday. By the way, I did get one, and I loved her so much. I mean, why would God listen to a 7-year-old anyway? I was happy if my favorite episode of Punky Brewster was on T.V. My priorities were not that great.

My next experience with loss was equally confusing and upsetting. My cousin Jimmy died in a car accident when I was just 14. He was in his 20s, and I always looked up to my older cousins. His mom and my mom were sisters. When I was younger, his mom would babysit for us. We would watch wrestling with him and his siblings. I remember one Christmas Eve, all of my older male cousins teased us relentlessly about liking the New Kids on the Block. They changed the lyrics of "Grandma Got Run Over By a Reindeer" to "New Kids on the Block Got Run Over by a Reindeer." We were livid. They thought it was hilarious. They were always teasing us and joking around. We had really happy memories of Jimmy from our childhood. I felt blessed to have had cousins that I loved so much.

I hadn't known a young person who died before. I always thought it was one of those things that was tragic when it happened, but it didn't happen to you or your family. It was just something you read about in the newspaper or saw on TV. This death was especially traumatic for me because it was the first time I thought about my own mortality. I know that seems silly. Of course, I knew that I would die someday. I just assumed it wouldn't be until I was very old because that's the way things worked. Remember God, 45 is NOT old. Now I knew someone who died young. It could happen to me, or worse, it could happen to another family member. What if it happened to one of my siblings? This became very real for me. I will never forget hearing the screams from my aunt when she first went in to view her son. It's a sound you don't soon forget.

It was a helpless feeling because I wanted to be able to take away her pain, yet there was nothing that I or anyone else could say or do that would ease the heartbreak. I will always believe that it is the cruelest thing on Earth to lose a child. I know there is a higher purpose in it, but I have yet to figure out what it is. I think that might be my first question to God when I get to the other side. That, and why did you listen to a stupid 7-year-old? The next major experience that I had with death is one that I wish I could completely erase from my memory. It was traumatic, and horrific, and still causes me nightmares even to this day.

My ex-husband and father of my children took his own life in 2020. I was teaching a class when I received a text from his brother asking me to call him as soon as possible. I immediately had a sinking feeling because I never got texts from his brother. We had been divorced for almost 18 years at that point. I knew something was wrong. When I called him, his voice sounded broken. He said, "My brother took his life last night." My kids were seniors in high school, and when I received the news, my daughter was sitting in my classroom, just feet away from me as I heard the words "took his own life." I had her as a student in my German class that year, and I had to spend 30 excruciating minutes acting as though nothing was wrong. I had to lie and say that it was my doctor on the phone confirming a prescription. I couldn't tell her the truth. I felt panic-stricken. I was sick to my stomach.

My head was spinning. I wanted to scream, I wanted to run, and most of all I wanted out of there. Time crawled for me at that moment. Unfortunately for me that day, both of my kids regularly came in and ate lunch in my room during 3rd Hour. Not only did I have to act normal in front of my daughter, but my son came in for lunch, and I still had to act as though I hadn't just heard the most gruesome news of my life. I had to endure 30 more minutes of agony. Yet again, time was my enemy. I wanted to throw up, yet I had to smile at them, knowing that in just a few hours I would shatter their hearts and change their lives forever. I watched as they laughed and giggled at each other. My heart was sinking further into my stomach. I was fighting back tears. How would I ever be able to tell them what happened? I hated this so much. It wasn't fair to them, and it wasn't fair that I had to be the one to tell them. I did not want to have to tell them. What would I even say? How could I break their hearts like that?.

This was my first year teaching at this school, and I didn't know what to do. I didn't have anyone that I trusted enough to go to with this news. I did the first thing my instincts said to do, which was to reach out to Mom. I texted her immediately. She tried to comfort me via text. I could tell that she was shocked and shaken up too. She told me to go home as soon as I could. I went down to the office to ask for a sub, and when I tried to explain why I needed to go home, I started sobbing uncontrollably. The secretary was so nice to me, yet I knew she was very uncomfortable too. She promised she would find me a sub and asked what else she could do. I said, "Nothing." I had to go home to prepare myself for how I would tell my children. Luckily, my mom and my brother left work early and came to be with me. We worked out a plan for how we could break the news gently. Spoiler alert, there is absolutely no way to do that...none whatsoever. It's going to suck. It's going to be awful. It doesn't matter what you say or do. There is absolutely no good way to tell your children that their father took his own life.

At that moment, I was so angry at him for being so selfish. He left me with a horrible mess to clean up. He left them with so much pain and confusion. How could he do this to them? What was he thinking? Why did this have to happen? At the same time, I was heartbroken for him. Things must have seemed inescapably awful to him for him to feel that he had no other choice. Even though I was angry, I was also grieving for a man that I once loved.

I felt so many emotions that day that ranged from anger and frustration to immense sadness. Thank goodness, I had a team of people who were sending me love and support. My head was foggy. I felt numb. I felt like I was sleepwalking through a horrific nightmare. I kept trying to jolt myself awake, only to realize that this wasn't a dream. This was real, and I had no idea how to navigate this.

Reluctantly, I called for an early dismissal for my children. I wanted them to stay at school as long as possible so that their lives could be normal for just a little while longer, and in all honesty, I was dreading having to break the news to them. I was so nervous, and I still felt like I was going to be sick. My school's secretary was worried that the kids might find out on Facebook or another social media platform, so she suggested I send them home early. They drove to school separately that day. My daughter came in first. When I told her the news, she let out the worst primal scream that I have ever heard, and she fell to the floor. The scream in and of itself was gut-wrenching and haunting. I can still hear it when I close my eyes at night. I don't ever want to hear that scream again. I wanted to hug her and take away her pain, but I knew I couldn't. There were no words that I could say and nothing that I could do that would provide comfort. It was the most helpless feeling in the world as a mom to watch her suffering and not to be able to stop it. You feel like a failure as a parent because it's your job to protect them, yet I couldn't protect them from this. Grief does not come with a shield.

My son took the early dismissal as his chance to start the weekend early. He went to hang out with his friends. I had to call him to come home. He came home about 20 minutes after my daughter. When we told him the news, he got sick. He sobbed, and again there was nothing that I could say or do that would ease his pain. It tore me to shreds to have to watch them experience this. It didn't get easier with time. The days and weeks that followed were horrendous. I didn't know what to do to help them, and they just seemed to be lost and in shock. When they finally felt strong enough to come back to school, COVID-19 hit. On one hand, it was a blessing for us because they were still struggling to be around people. Online classes were much easier for them to manage than being in person.

People mean well, but other kids would stare at them or ask them if they were OK. They just wanted to feel normal again. My son tried to be brave and go back to school a week after his dad's death, and in his first-hour class, they announced it was suicide prevention week. He didn't even make it an hour in school before he had to go home.

On the other hand, they missed out on prom and graduation because of Covid. My sweet babies should have been celebrating their senior year, prom, and going off to college, but instead, they were just in survival mode. It is an extremely difficult thing to lose a parent so young and in such a violent way.

I have lost many other beloved relatives in my life including my Grandma Oatman, my great aunt Betty, my aunt Kay, my cousin Debbie, and my Uncle Delmar to name a few. It's not that their deaths didn't affect me. They did, of course. Death is never easy, after all. It was just different. It didn't have the impact that those other deaths did. I didn't see those people every day, and they didn't die young or tragically. It doesn't matter how it comes, though. Death is still difficult, and you will never be fully prepared for it, no matter how or when it comes to visit.

My hope in writing this book is that by sharing my story, I can help you heal. I hope you know that you are not alone. I know how much grief hurts. I know how debilitating it can be. I know that if you are reading this right now, you are probably in a lot of pain. You are most likely stuck in this battle, feeling as though your life lost its meaning or direction. I understand. I have questioned myself and this process more in the past year than I ever have in my entire life. What I can tell you is this. Grief has no expiration date. There's no magic pill you can take. You can't decide when and where it will hit you. It's a process. While you can't always decide how or when it will hit you, you can decide that you will choose to process it.

I have met so many people who don't deal with their grief, and their emotions come out in very toxic ways. Pushing down your feelings does not make them go away. It simply makes you miserable, and it can even make you physically sick. My goal is to give you the tools you need so that when you are ready, you can work through your grief with grace. You are not alone. Millions of people experience grief every single day.

Anyone who doesn't experience grief is not human, in my opinion. Grief is a natural part of life; no one escapes this world without experiencing it at some point. What I choose to hold onto is the thought that the bigger your pain and grief are, the stronger your love is. I think that's a beautiful thing. It's proof that love is very real, and it's worth the pain in the end to experience it. You were blessed to have known a love so strong. I hope that it comforts you to know this one thing–you **can** heal, and you **can** go on without your loved one. The truth is that your loved one is still very much with you and a part of your life. They never really leave us. They simply take on a new form. Love never dies. It is eternal. I will show you how to feel the love that your person still has for you, and I will help you see that they are still around you all the time. You will get through this, and I hope to help you. I will show you how to process your grief so that it doesn't keep you stuck anymore, and I'll help you see that there are still so many more beautiful things in life out there for you if you simply choose to see them.

CHAPTER 2
WHAT IS THIS GRIEF STUFF ANYWAY

What exactly is grief, and why is it so difficult? I mean, we know that grief usually means sadness, but it is so much more than that. What is it really all about? What does it entail? According to the Oxford dictionary, the definition of grief is "deep sorrow, especially that caused by someone's death," although grief doesn't occur only when we experience a physical death. We can experience grief at the loss of a relationship, a friendship, a job, or even at the loss of health or vitality. Grief comes from so many different sources, and we experience it multiple times throughout our lives. It is a natural part of the human experience. No one escapes life without coming face to face with grief. Grief is a common thread that binds us all. Grief even affects the natural world too. Animals also experience grief. It tears me up every time I see a video on TikTok of an animal whose owner has passed away. They grieve for us, too. Grief affects every living thing on this planet. That is why it is so important to understand it more thoroughly.

Because there are so many different sources of grief, it affects us differently from one instance to another. For example, you may lose a job and feel sad or lost. Maybe it only lasts until you find your next job. On the other hand, if you lost the love of your life, it might hurt so deeply that you can't function. You may have this deep pain, and it may last for many years. Both of those are examples of grief, but you can see how one has a much larger and more lasting impact on someone's life. It doesn't matter what the cause of your grief is. It is painful nonetheless, and you should never downplay yours or someone else's grief. An important step is to accept and honor your grief. Do not ever allow anyone to diminish your grief. You are entitled to feel anything you feel. You have to acknowledge and process your emotions in order to truly begin to heal. I've actually heard people tell others that they need to get over something. That is the worst thing you can say to someone, and it is cruel and false. Yes, we need to work through our grief in order to process it in a healthy way, but you never just get over it. It takes time and work to get through grief.

One thing I would like to mention is that there is no wrong or right way to grieve. There are ways to deal with grief that are healthier than others; however, every person is different, which means every person's grief journey will be different as well. I would also like to point out that grief does not have an expiration date. Do not let anyone tell you to get over it, or that you should be feeling better by now. It doesn't work that way. Wouldn't it be great if it did? I wish you could push a button and make these horrible feelings go away or swallow a pill and forget everything.

That would be nice. Hey grief, you're kind of an asshole, so go away. How amazing would that be, but you absolutely can't do that. There is no way to truly escape your pain. You can't pay someone money to erase your memories. You can only do that in the movies.

This brings me to another very critical point. I need to emphasize the importance of feeling your emotions. You can try to ignore your feelings. You can numb them with substances, or try to outrun them by staying busy, or you can even pick up unhealthy habits. I know of someone who got into a very unhealthy and toxic relationship because they were looking for momentary happiness and a distraction. If that person hadn't been trying to outrun their emotions or fill the void they felt in their life, they would have realized that this person/relationship was extremely unhealthy and not destined to last. I think when we try to avoid how we feel, we end up doing things we would not normally do. We are desperately searching for a way to feel better. None of that works, though. You may even feel like pushing people away because you don't want to be reminded of your loss or have to answer any questions. Maybe being around your loved ones reminds you of the one who is missing, but pushing away your family and friends is also not the answer. Sure, it may seem as though it's working in the short term, but believe me, those feelings do not go away until you process them. They are only pushed deeper into your subconscious. Your body still knows that those feelings are there waiting for you to acknowledge them. Plus, you could be hurting others simply because you are hurting. This only causes more pain all around.

You may be wondering what happens when you don't process your grief. Nothing good is the short answer. Here are just some of the things that could happen if you don't deal with your pain properly. First, you will probably ugly cry after drinking, because although alcohol numbs us at first, it also makes those feelings come out. It will probably happen in public because we generally go out to have a drink. That is awkward and embarrassing. Not that I would know. Second, you end up having emotional explosions over things that are not really a big deal because you are pushing so much down deep inside. It has to come out in some way. Think of the straw that broke the camel's back, if you will. It is usually the people closest to us that we hurt when we do this. There is a saying that goes, "If you don't heal yourself, you will bleed all over people who didn't cut you." That is most definitely true. We tend to take out our emotions on those who are closest to us because we feel safe with them. Third, You may damage the relationships you have with the people in your life because you aren't making good choices. If you are numbing yourself with drugs or alcohol, and you are avoiding your friends and family, or if you are generally making poor life choices, it could impact your current relationships. You know, you are bleeding all over those who didn't cut you.

Furthermore, excessive drinking and drug use is detrimental to your health and can kill you. Fourth, and this is the most important reason you should definitely process your grief–you will get physically sick if you aren't allowing your feelings to come up. Unprocessed emotions become stuck in the body and they cause many physical problems.

As a Reiki practitioner, I often see clients who are experiencing physical pain or other symptoms. Before I do a Reiki session with a client, I connect to their energy. When I connect to my client's energy, I am able to connect to the physical symptoms as well as different emotions that they are experiencing. For example, I had a client who had throat cancer. This client came to me to help alleviate the side effects of chemo. When I met with this client and connected to the client's energy, I received the message that he had a blocked throat chakra. He wasn't speaking his truth or setting healthy boundaries for himself. I told my client what I was getting. The client told me that there was conflict with a person in their life. This client felt the person was disrespecting them. Those emotions of resentment and hurt showed up as a physical ailment in the body. Most people think that if they ignore their emotions, they will get over them. Um, no, you obviously do not just get over it by ignoring it. Your body doesn't lie. Unprocessed emotions become energy that gets stuck or trapped in the body. When emotions are left unprocessed, you will see it manifest into physical or psychological problems.

Ignoring your pain will only make your grief worse, and it prolongs the experience. That may seem counterintuitive. If I ignore my pain, how am I prolonging it? At first ignoring your emotional pain may seem to make you feel better; however, those emotions will come out. Isn't it better to decide that you are going to deliberately process them when, where, and how you want to? Let me give you an example. After my mom passed away, we had a really difficult time. At first, my siblings and I were trying to be strong for everyone else, and we had so many things to take care of that we never really had time to grieve properly. A few weeks after my mom died, we went to a wine tasting at my friend's house. After about two glasses of wine, I looked up and saw my sister begin to cry. She whispered, "I miss mom." She then started sobbing uncontrollably, which made us all cry until we were all sobbing (like completely ugly crying) too. We all looked like we had just been through a natural disaster. What a fun wine party! My point is that emotions left unchecked will come out at the most embarrassingly inopportune times. Luckily, my friend is super chill, and he loved my mom too. He totally understood and was kind enough to never speak of it again. Come to think of it, though, he's never invited me back to another wine party. I wonder why.

Why do so many people try to avoid their emotions? Wouldn't it be so much better if we just let it out? The easy and most obvious answer to that question is yes. It would be so much better if we processed our emotions. It seems like this would be an easy solution, but many people have difficulty expressing their emotions. This seems to be an epidemic for our and previous generations. Think about how many times you have been ghosted in life. There are a multitude of adults running around not expressing how they feel, and it isn't really that difficult to understand why. My generation was the generation of latchkey kids. We came home from school and took care of ourselves. Many of us were told as children, "Stop crying, or I will give you something to cry about." At least, I was. Perhaps you heard, "Don't be such a cry baby," or "Suck it up, Buttercup." Our parents' generation of parenting was so sweet, warm, and fuzzy, was it not?! They literally had to air a commercial on television asking our parents if they knew where we were? Do you remember that? It's 10:00. Do you know where your children are? I mean really? Not exactly hands-on or touchy-feely parenting.

Don't misunderstand me. I think our parents tried their best. The problem is that because of this lack of touchy-feely parenting, we associate crying or expressing emotion as a bad thing. It made us look weak, or worse, it made us seem needy. Maybe we felt like we were a burden to others when we expressed our needs. I know when my mom said things like that, she wasn't trying to make me feel bad. She just wanted me to stop crying over something stupid because, as kids, we tend to cry over silly things sometimes. I used to cry if she made my sister and I split a soda, and I had to drink out of a cup instead of the can. I totally understand why she would tell me to stop crying. That's a ridiculous reason to cry, but as children, we don't understand that. We want our needs to be met. In that instance, I wasn't getting my needs met. The tricky part is that it teaches us subconscious lessons. It teaches us things like don't show your emotions, or don't ask for what you need because it isn't safe. You can understand why we have so many issues today. For many people, expressing emotion does not come easily or naturally. That doesn't mean you can't learn how. It's like learning to ride a bike. All it takes is practice, or at least someone running behind you, pushing you and then letting you fall. Maybe that's why I don't trust anyone.

My point in all of this is that you have to process your emotions. It's healthy and natural for you to feel your feelings. Now I sound like Stuart Smalley. I keep dating myself with these references, and I am having the Millennials running to Google to figure out who I am talking about. (Go look it up. It is hilarious.) Well, you're good enough and smart enough. It's true though.

Holding things inside is not going to help you. You will feel better if you choose to work through your grief. So, that leads to the big question. How do you work through your grief? What is that even supposed to look like? That is a great question, and I am so glad you asked it. What should your grief journey look like? Let's talk about the stages of grief for a moment.

It was long a common belief that there are five stages of grief, and that you go through each of these stages throughout the grief process. In her 1969 book "On Death and Dying," psychiatrist Elisabeth Kubler-Ross identified the five stages of grief as denial, anger, bargaining, depression, and acceptance. This theory was later reimagined to include the seven stages of grief. Those seven stages are shock and denial, pain and guilt, anger and bargaining, depression, the upward turn, reconstructing and working through, and acceptance and hope. While I believe that these theories are valuable in explaining what grief can look like, it's important to understand that you can't actually put a label on where someone is on their grief journey. The other problem I have with these theories is that people often misinterpret that grief is linear. Some people believe that you go through the stages in order. Based on my own experience, I can 100 percent tell you that grief is not linear. There are days when I feel that I am experiencing three of these stages at the same time. There are also days when I thought I experienced my anger, and then I hear or read something and feel angry all over again. And some days, I don't even know what it is that I am feeling. Some people skip stages all together, too. Because you are a unique individual, your grief journey is unique to you. Wouldn't it be nice if we could say today I will go through anger, and then tomorrow I will experience guilt, and I will move through each of these stages and after a month, I will feel better. It would be great if we could label everything and tuck it away neatly in boxes, but the truth is that grief is very messy and unpredictable. Sorry to all of you out there with OCD. Grief will drive you insane.

Grief can be very confusing. Some days I didn't even understand what I was feeling. I couldn't describe it to you if I tried, and none of the labels above describe it either. The best label I can think of is the nothing void. Nothing excited me. I wanted to do nothing and be nothing. I just didn't care much. How do you really label all the different combinations of heavy emotions, anyway? I think we try to label everything too much as it is. I still have days when if someone asks me how I am, I simply say, "I'm here." I do not know how to answer that question. By the way, that is a question that I have come to hate. I don't think we should ask people how they are when they have lost someone. What are you supposed to say? The world sucks, life sucks, you suck and I don't want to be here anymore. I mean, what do people actually want you to say? I've been so happy since my loved one died! I didn't realize how amazing life could be without them. If you've ever said that, you're a terrible person. I'm kidding, of course. All anyone usually says is, "I'm fine." I think that is all anyone wants you to say. We know that this is the furthest thing from the truth, but it's easier just to say that. At least if you say that you are doing ok, people leave you alone. If you say that you are not doing well, people try to follow it up with more annoying and probing questions.

Just leave me alone, please!! Conversely, some people may want others to ask them how they are doing. They may feel better talking about it.

For me, it was difficult to have to express how I was feeling when I didn't even know myself. You will be a jumble of emotions, and that is perfectly fine. It doesn't feel fine, but it does mean that you are normal. For the purpose of helping you understand grief, I am going to go through each stage in the seven stages of the grief process in the next few chapters. Know that you may or may not be experiencing these emotions, and that is perfectly OK too. These stages are not finite, and as I stated earlier, grief is often a messy process. Some people skip the stages all together. Some people find that they go back and forth many times between each stage. It's not as easy as putting our emotions into tiny little boxes. Some days we will feel better, and some days the waves of grief almost knock us out of our shoes. Remember that it's important to have grace and patience with yourself during this process. You may find that unexpected things trigger you...like seeing your loved one's name on your Netflix account, or going to the doctor and seeing that your loved one was your emergency contact. I am no longer allowed at my doctor's office because I ugly cried there for this very reason. Also, other people may say very stupid things to you that trigger you. It's always fun when I run into someone who didn't know my mom died. Then I have to tell them that she passed away. I can tell that they feel horrible for not knowing and making me tell them that she died. They are also super uncomfortable. Of course, you could handle it like my brother. Someone asked him how my mom was doing, and he responded, "She's in

Heaven." We all looked at him in disbelief. Then he said, "I don't know why I said it like that." It did cause us to burst out into waves of laughter, so I guess it was comic relief. It can be really traumatic when something like that happens. You never know what to say. When it does, and it will, give them grace. People are idiots. Just remember that it is OK to not be OK. You don't have to know that everything will be OK, either. Just trust this process and be willing to explore the idea that you can and will heal. You will feel better eventually, and there are still beautiful things waiting for you.

CHAPTER 3

SHOCK AND DENIAL: THE FIRST WAVE OF GRIEF

The first stage of grief is shock and denial. This stage may be particularly prevalent if the death or loss you experienced was sudden or unexpected, but it isn't limited to those kinds of losses. My mother was diagnosed with pancreatic cancer in June 2020, and she passed away in January 2022. She didn't die suddenly for unknown reasons. We knew this could be the outcome, yet it still seemed unexpected, and we were still shocked by her passing. In fact, I'm still shocked to this very day that she died. It's been over two years later, and there are days that I still don't believe she is gone. I will have a dream about her where she seems very much alive. I have entire conversations with her in my dreams that feel so lifelike. Then I wake up and realize all over again that she is gone and not coming back. It feels like a punch to the gut every time.

Up until November 2021, my mom had been doing better. Her doctors had told us that they really thought she might be able to beat her cancer. If I am being honest, she probably would have survived if she had been sick at any other time in history. Covid delayed a lot of her treatment and caused so many issues for us. We had gathered so much hope. In fact, there are still days that I don't understand why she didn't survive. I know that her diagnosis was a tough one, but I didn't expect her to go as quickly as she did.

She rang the bell at her last chemo treatment and was told she was cancer free. Although we knew she was sick, we had no idea how bad it would get. It's unimaginable to me that she's gone. I will see a picture of her, and it's almost as if I'm reminded once again that she is no longer here, and I feel those initial feelings of sadness and emptiness once more.

She has been gone for a while, yet I still have dreams where I tell her we found a cure for her, and then I realize that it doesn't matter because she's already dead. I even have the thought that she doesn't have her body because we cremated her. It's so strange. There are still people walking around out there who didn't know she died. I have to tell them, and they look shocked and embarrassed that they didn't know. I can tell that they feel badly for making me tell them that she passed away because maybe it reopens that wound for me. I still feel like I will wake up from this nightmare one day, and she will be standing in front of me. We will laugh about how silly this all was. It can take a while for the shock to wear off. When shock hits me, I have to tell myself that my mom is in a much better place. It's difficult for me, but it would be selfish of me to bring her back because she was suffering so much.

What might it feel like to be in this particular stage of grief? What does shock and denial look like? It often looks or feels like numbness and brain fog. It can also look like avoidance or procrastination. The loss of a loved one can be overwhelming, and the first few days and weeks are filled with activities that keep you busy. You have so much to do that it is like running on autopilot. You simply have to get through what has to be done. It almost feels like you are dissociating. I know I felt detached from my body. It almost felt like I was walking through a dream. I believe this is a coping mechanism that the brain uses to help shield you from the pain. Plus, with all the work it takes to plan a funeral, you feel bombarded by responsibilities. For me, it felt like I barely had time to think or even breathe. That is a very normal part of the grief process.

My grief journey started long before my mom actually died. It started when we found out that she had cancer. I think I was in denial for most of that. I just knew she was going to recover. I didn't even try to think about the possibility of her dying. It was not an option for me. In fact, when she would try to bring up what to do if she died, I would tell her to stop talking about it. I didn't want to even think about the possibility of her death. I couldn't imagine not having her around. I didn't want that to even be a consideration. I tried to avoid thinking about the worst that could happen, and it made me angry when others brought it up because I felt like that was a sign that they were giving up. As long as I had hope, everything would be ok.

The truly painful part of the grieving process began for me when my mom was actively dying. Until that time, I wouldn't face the fact that she was dying because I wholeheartedly believed that she would be able to beat this cancer. The day before she died was so intense that it will live in my memory forever. My mom had been hospitalized for a massive infection. She had been there for a week. The doctors couldn't decide what to do for her. They decided to try a procedure. One doctor didn't want to do it, and one did. We had been in a battle all week over what they were going to do for her. We were frustrated and exhausted. The Saturday before she died, my brother woke me up at 6 a.m. The hospital called and it wasn't good news. They wanted my siblings and I to come to the hospital for a meeting. My mom had undergone the procedure that they didn't want to do, which was to drain the fluids from her infection. The procedure sent the infection out into her body, which caused sepsis. Her blood pressure had dropped overnight. We were told in that meeting that my mom would most likely never regain consciousness. The doctors did not think that my mom would wake up or be able to fight off the infection that she had. We had to start making some very difficult decisions.

She did not regain consciousness after her procedure. They were keeping her blood pressure steady through medication. They felt that once they turned off the medication, she would pass away. Her organs were already beginning to shut down. They wanted to know what our wishes were for her. Since my brother had power of attorney, he had to make the final choice. They told us to take the rest of that day to decide what we wanted to do. What we decided to do was to put her on comfort care in order to allow everyone time to come and say goodbye. We were still clinging on to some sort of hope that she would pull through, even though now I see that this was futile. The brain will allow you to think interesting things in order to protect you from the pain. The hospital allowed us to invite anyone who wanted to say goodbye to her to come and see her. We could all have our time with her, and then we would let her pass peacefully.

We were so busy trying to call everyone making sure we didn't miss anyone who might want to see her, and then we were comforting all the people who came to say goodbye, that we didn't have time to really process or accept what was happening. After her friends and family said their goodbyes, we were able to have our time with her, just us. We each stood around her bedside. I held one hand and one of my siblings held her other hand. We told her we loved her, tried to sing a little to her again, and told her it was ok to go. It was a bittersweet moment. It was terrible to have to let her go, yet it was beautiful that we were there to witness it. It's both a blessing and a curse at the same time to watch someone take their last breath. On one hand, it is a beautiful moment to know that she was transitioning to a better place, and we were witness to that. On the other hand, we were losing one of the most important people in our lives, and we would never see her on this Earth again.

After she took her last breath, we were inundated with all the things that had to be done. I remember not knowing what to expect at first. The hospital staff told us we had to sign a form to release her body to the funeral home. I am so thankful that our dear family friend Lori stayed with us the whole time to help us with the planning. I had no idea what happens after you die in a hospital. We had to call the funeral home, pick out an outfit, find pictures, write the obituary, plan the service and meal, and create a video for her service. There was so much to do the week following her death and during her services that I never really had time to truly process what had just happened. I didn't have time to feel much of anything. I was too busy trying to take care of everything that needed to be done. I was numb and in a trance-like state. It was one of those times when I know I ate, I know I got dressed, I know I talked to people, but I remember nothing. At her wake, I was comforting family, friends, and her former students, most of whom were sobbing. We were so busy comforting everyone else, that we didn't think of our own grief. I think a lot of people experience this. We didn't truly have time to understand and process our pain until after the dust settled.

When my ex-husband died, I was very much in denial. There were so many times that I thought to myself that maybe he faked his own death. It was honestly not out of the realm of possibility with him. Because of Covid, he was cremated immediately. My kids didn't get to go see his body because they would have had to embalm him and probably make him look better. That would have cost more money, and it wasn't what he wanted, so they decided not to do it. All of us, including my kids, wondered if this was some elaborate scheme he had cooked up. I think we just couldn't believe that he had really done this. It was a little escape from reality to believe that he had orchestrated some elaborate ruse to trick us into thinking that he was dead. We finally had to come to terms with reality. He was gone. It was true. He had done this terrible thing. I think part of the reason we wanted to believe that he had faked his death is because it was easier to believe that than to believe that he had passed in such a horrific way.

His passing left so many holes. The kids never really got closure with him. They were hurting and in so much pain, and they still had all of their belongings at his house. There were so many things left up in the air. Because the kids had turned 18 a few weeks before he died, there was no financial help for them. I was receiving child support, and it just suddenly stopped. In fact, one of the things that makes me sick to my stomach is that my last text message to him was asking if he was going to Venmo me that week. Obviously, if I had any idea what was happening, my text would have been something totally different. It was a habit that I had to send him that same text every other week as a reminder for him. We would often joke about it. Now, that was the last text he got from me. I felt horrible about that. It really was tough financially for us, though. This was my kids' senior year. We were looking at colleges. How would we afford this? I had started a college savings fund for them, but I was the only one contributing to it. I started it too late. Would it be enough? The kids also now needed counseling. We found a wonderful place, but their insurance did not cover it. I had taken a pay cut when I switched schools. I was super stressed about how we would make it financially.

Aside from the questions about finances, there were questions about how my kids would heal. They needed help getting through this emotional trauma. How would they ever adjust to this loss? Would they ever feel whole again? Would they be able to forgive him or forgive themselves because I know they wanted to blame themselves? Would they forgive me? I chose this person who then created so much pain for them. I couldn't stop the bad behavior that they had to endure from him. They were hurting so much, how could they heal? Would they recover from this? I barely slept at night because these questions filled my brain. I hurt for them. I worried about them. My whole family worried about them. We loved them so much, and to see them in this much pain was unbearable.

We did eventually come to terms with his death, and after counseling, it got a little easier to accept. We found a great support group and through that group, we found an amazing counselor too. The shock phase does eventually wear off, and when it does, you will need some support too. I think counseling or coaching is always a great idea (if you find one who is a good fit for you). Family and friends can also be a huge support. After the initial shock wears off, you will need people to talk to. You need someone or something to help you start processing your emotions.

After the tumultuous experience of the first few weeks wanes and reality sets in, you will finally have to start facing the truth. We had to face the fact that my kids' father and my mother were not coming back. It isn't easy when you finally realize that this is permanent. You know your life will never be the same, but it is important that you face it. Imagining that it didn't happen or walking through life in a fog won't make the pain go away, and it is no way to live. When I was married to my ex, I became numb to everything around me. My ex used to say cruel things to me just to try to gain control of me. It used to hurt my feelings a lot in the beginning, and I never understood why he said those things. It got so bad that I started dissociating. I stopped caring about what he did or said, but the problem was I stopped caring about everything. I just numbed myself so that I couldn't feel the pain when he criticized me. A huge issue with that was that my kids were only a year old. I was missing out on memories with them because I was a walking zombie. That wasn't fair to them or to myself. In trying to avoid my pain, I was also avoiding making beautiful new memories with my family.

Avoidance, shutting down emotionally, and procrastination are other ways this grief can manifest itself. After my mom died, I really needed to be around people. It comforted me. My brother was the total opposite. He avoided family like the plague. He didn't want to be around any of the family. At least, not if we were going to be talking about my mom. He didn't want anyone talking about her, and he procrastinated doing things that he was normally always on top of. He even said to me once, "I wish everyone would stop trying to make me sad." Our relationship really suffered after my mom's death. It's hard to be around someone who doesn't want you around. My son also wanted to avoid people after his dad died. People were a reminder that life wasn't normal anymore. He didn't want to have to talk about it, and he didn't want anyone asking him questions. He shut down when it came to school, and to say he procrastinated when doing his homework would be an understatement. I had such a difficult time getting him to turn in his work. It was tough for me because I understood why he didn't want to do it, but as his mom, I had to ensure that he graduated from high school. Avoidance and isolation are just some of the ways that people cope with pain and trauma.

Avoidance can be useful when it is used in the short term to help you get through a particular situation. For example, when I learned that my children's father passed away, I had to ignore my feelings in order to get through the rest of the hour with them. They were sitting just feet away, and I had to push down my feelings so that they did not notice that anything was wrong. In that particular instance, avoidance helped me get through a difficult moment. When used over a period of time, however, avoidance actually becomes a negative coping skill. Avoidance behaviors are things like using substances to numb oneself, constantly saying "I'm fine," cutting yourself off from family and friends, engaging in unhealthy behavior, staying busy, or even cutting oneself.

These behaviors become negative coping mechanisms when used over a long period of time. They prevent a person from learning how to properly heal from pain and trauma. Avoidance does exactly what the word says. It causes a person to avoid the healing process entirely. It is extremely important not to avoid your feelings. We talked earlier about how it can lead to illness in the body. I know that pain hurts. I know you don't want to feel bad. No one really enjoys feeling bad, except maybe the Debbie Downers in life. The harsh reality is that sometimes you just have to feel it. There is truly no solid way to avoid those painful emotions. It's like pulling off a Band-Aid. It's easier in the long run if you rip it off immediately. It hurts, but the pain subsides quicker. That is how it is when you allow yourself to experience your emotions. You have to feel it to heal it. That is the only way you can begin to recover.

Remember the statement from earlier... "If you don't heal your wounds, you will bleed all over people who didn't cut you." That statement is so powerful, and it is very true. My brother was hurting so much after my mom died that he actually began hurting others. He didn't realize that he was hurting anyone because I was the only person who would tell him that he was hurting my feelings. I don't think he realized the damage he did. It hurts to have a family member become a stranger to you. It hurts when a family member shuts you out of their life. Furthermore, it is extremely painful when your loved one is no longer in your photos or going to your family events because that family member can't handle or doesn't want to deal with the pain it might cause them. He missed out on so many beautiful memories, all because he wanted to avoid the painful ones. I totally understand the reasoning behind this. This is how I dealt with the pain my ex caused me when I was in my 20s. I had to learn how to process it. I learned that until I did, I would be stuck on autopilot in life, missing out on all the beautiful memories, or worse, numbing myself and feeling nothing at all. That is no way to live. It is miserable.

The good news is that my brother and I did eventually start mending our relationship. We both sought counseling, and it helped tremendously. The tough thing about grief is that no person or thing can save you from it. You have to save yourself. You do that by healing. Besides, you can't save anyone who isn't ready to heal. Facing reality is tough, but it is the only way to work through your grief so that you can feel better and start living life again.

Being numb only works for so long. Yes, you might not feel the pain from the loss of your loved one, but you will also miss the joy that comes from the beautiful experiences in life like the birth of a new baby, laughing with a friend, or seeing the magnificence of nature. Plus, you have people here who still need you. You still have a purpose in life. You can't stop living because you still have so much more to do. Your loved one would not want you to stop living, either. They would want you to go on and live your best life. Your best life is not one where you are walking around comatose. You deserve to feel love, joy, happiness, and above all, peace. You still have so much more of life to discover. Don't let it end here. Your journey is still ongoing. You need to find the strength to keep living knowing that your loved one is right here with you watching over you.

The best way to move forward is to be fully present in each moment. Don't disconnect from the world. It doesn't mean you have to focus on the death of your loved one. You can be present by going outside for a walk. Notice the trees, listen to the birds, and look at the sky. Find beautiful things to appreciate in life. If you drink coffee, go outside and enjoy your coffee in nature. Enjoy the flavor of your coffee or the way it smells. I personally love the smell of fresh coffee. Notice the pretty flowers, smell their fragrance, and listen to the sounds. Connecting to nature can be very healing. Do things for yourself that make you feel good and that are healthy for you. Go get a massage, a facial, or a manicure. Read a good book…you know, like this one. Watch a funny movie. Self-care is so important right now, and it is the one thing that we tend to neglect the most when we are grieving. As much as I know you probably don't want to, you need to make sure you are eating well, sleeping, and taking care of your emotional health. I like listening to podcasts and YouTube videos that are inspirational or informative.

It lifts my mood. I know of a good podcast called "Awaken Your Inner Awesomeness." The host is a pretty cool chick. There are several podcasts on grief that are excellent. "Grief with Grace" is a podcast hosted by my friend Lori Latimer. She always has helpful topics around grief. I also like listening to uplifting music and singing really loudly. I don't care if I sound good or not. It's fun. You are allowed to have fun again. You are allowed to live again.

Start doing the things you would normally do again. You may have to force yourself to do these things again at first, but once you do, you will see that it will help. Having daily routines helps tremendously. You will start to slowly feel better. Self-care was something that I stopped doing after my mom died. I didn't realize it at first.

I knew I didn't feel great, but I just assumed it was because I was grieving. What I didn't notice was that I had let my self-care practice go. I couldn't tell you the last time that I exercised, and I used to love that. I used to listen to affirmations in the morning. I stopped doing that too. I had to make myself schedule time in my day for myself. I made myself take time off to do absolutely anything that I enjoyed. Remember to take baby steps and be gentle with yourself during this process. You are very fragile right now, and that is OK. You have permission to take it slowly. In no way should you feel like you have to completely be normal again after the loss of a loved one. Maybe add in one self-care routine at a time. When you feel better, add in something else.

Journaling is a great way to start the healing process. If you don't feel like talking to people, then write down what you are feeling. No one has to see your writing. Then you don't have to avoid people when you see them because you can tell them you are processing your feelings privately. I think it is perfectly acceptable to tell friends and family that you would rather not talk about your grief. As long as you are processing it, you don't have to process it in public or with others. You can do it by yourself. If you set that boundary with your family, then you won't feel the need to avoid them. Journaling is really a fantastic tool. It's a way for you to declutter your brain, and it helps you process what you are feeling at the same time. I know that not everyone enjoys writing. I have had several clients who rolled their eyes at me when I said they needed to get a journal. They don't like writing. I understand that. You can also just say out loud how you are feeling. When we speak it or write it, we are allowing it to get out of our heads and bodies. If you need to cry or scream, do it. How do you think those emotions are getting out...oh yeah, by getting out? Let all of that stuff out. Own it. You can say, "Today, I'm mad. I don't understand why this had to happen. Why am I still here?" Whatever you have to say...say it. You will feel better after expressing it. By being present and working through your pain, that numbness will fade. It will get easier to manage your emotions. You just have to have some tools to help you do it. Once you do, you won't bleed all over those who didn't cut you anymore. You will see that life is still full of possibilities. Beautiful experiences are still coming your way. Just wait and see.

You didn't come here to walk through life in an empty void. You came here to experience so many things. You still can. You made beautiful memories before, and you will again. Your loved one does not want to see you suffer. They want you to continue to live your life to the fullest and experience new things. After my mom passed, we decided to take a vacation. We would normally go on vacation with her. We could have said, "No, we can't ever take a vacation again because she isn't here to go with us." My mom would not have wanted that. Instead, we planned the vacation and made her a part of it with us. We took some of her ashes and spread them while we were there. We laughed about how she would have reacted to some of the things that happened to us.

We had to cram 13 people and all of our luggage into a van that had no storage space. Everyone had luggage sitting on his or her lap. It was so uncomfortable, and we laughed the entire way to our hotel. We knew my mom would have been rolling her eyes at us. We would never have had those beautiful memories if we had decided to stop living. Live your life, plan that next vacation, and keep going. You deserve to be happy again. Don't feel guilty for wanting to be happy again. We're going to address that guilt in the next chapter. Remember that if you get the choice to sit it out or dance in life, I hope you always choose to dance.

CHAPTER 4
GUILT: SHOULD-ING ALL OVER YOURSELF

uilt is a very common stage in the grief process. I like to call it the should-ing all over yourself stage because it is during this stage that we start thinking of all the things that we should have done for our loved ones. Whether we feel like there were things we could have done to save them, or maybe we just regret that we didn't express to them how much we loved them or spend enough time with them. Should-ing all over ourselves is when we beat ourselves up over what we think we should have done. This is very common to experience after the loss of a loved one. I know I experienced a lot of guilt. Some people are so hard on themselves and will find any excuse to feel guilty.

I am no exception to this. Guilt is an emotion that took a strong hold of me when my mom died. I felt extremely guilty for not trying to do more to help my mom than I did. I felt guilty for telling her that she wasn't eating enough and wasn't trying to help herself. I was ashamed that I had told her that she had the wrong mindset. I was often frustrated with her because I believed that she was not trying hard enough. Looking back, I see that you can't tell anyone how to live their life. My mom was very stubborn, and she was going to fight this illness on her own terms. She was going to do exactly what she wanted to do, whether we liked it or not. I had to accept the fact that I had done everything humanly possible to save my mom. I know that she handled her illness to the best of her ability. It was wrong of me to assume that she could have handled it better because I hadn't been through what she had. Believe me when I tell you that we fought hard. I watched cancer documentaries. I read books on it. I bought a juicer, consulted private holistic practitioners...you name it, and we tried it. I was determined to kill off this horrible disease. The amount of research that I did was only matched by the amount of guilt I felt when it didn't work. My aunt said something just a few weeks after her passing that brought me a little comfort. She said, "Lissa, I've never seen anyone fight as hard for her as you did."

I know in my heart of hearts that I did enough, but that is the interesting thing about grief–it makes us believe all kinds of things that aren't true. It amplifies those feelings of guilt. In my case, I always felt like I could have done more. I mean, I didn't buy a red light therapy mat. What if I had done that? Would she still be here today? No, I don't think she would still be here today if I had done that. The truth is that chemotherapy is what ultimately killed my mom. All of the preventative treatments we were giving her were worthless because the chemo was counteracting everything. There was nothing more we could have done that would have saved my mom. This is just a way that our brain tries to process grief. This is why I refer to it as the should-ing on yourself stage.

I should have gone to visit more, or I should have said I love you more, or fill in the blank with whatever you think you should have done differently.

Maybe you didn't go to the hospital to visit enough, maybe you could have spent more time with that loved one, maybe you think you should have seen warning signs of their illness sooner, or maybe you think there were more things you should have tried. It doesn't matter what the guilt is about. It is still a very tricky emotion. Even if you think your loved one was upset with you for not doing enough, you need to forgive yourself and have self-compassion. What I have learned is that when we cross over to the other side, we no longer carry those negative emotions. Your loved one has let it go, and so should you. Please stop beating yourself up for what you think you should have done.

I know this is easier said than done. It was a difficult thing for me to do when my ex-husband died. I felt guilty about his death for many reasons. My kids were not speaking to him at the time he died, and although they had very good reason to disconnect from him, I still felt sorry for him. I can't imagine not speaking to my children. He had withdrawn from many people in his life. I felt guilty that my children would have to grow up without a dad. Until my mom died, I didn't truly realize how painful losing a parent is. I tried to sympathize with them, but I had no idea how they were actually feeling. I just didn't get it until I experienced the same kind of loss. Maybe you feel that others don't understand your loss either. The truth is that they probably don't. Until you experience it firsthand, it is difficult to empathize with loss. I often thought about whether I could have said or done something to help my ex, but I know that I wouldn't have changed the outcome. It was almost as if he knew this was his destiny. He used to talk about that when we were together, but I didn't want to hear it. It was too gruesome to think about, and I never really believed he would do it.

When someone has made the decision to end their life, it is shocking, hurtful, and devastating. It is also extremely difficult for most people to understand. It feels like it goes against nature. We aren't supposed to take our own lives, right? Every religion preaches that it is a major sin. I used to feel that way too, until I heard it spoken about from a different perspective. We attended a support group for families of suicide victims, and something the counselor said stuck with me. She said mental illness is a disease. We don't punish people for having cancer, Some people survive cancer and some don't. Mental illness is no different. When you receive the proper treatment, your chances of survival increase significantly. Unfortunately, most people do not get the proper treatment, or the process is so slow and difficult that it is too late for them. Mental health is still considered a stigma in our society, even though the number of people who experience mental illness is rapidly increasing. It should be treated in the same way you would treat anyone else who has a disease. The unfortunate truth is that treating mental illness takes time, money, and patience. Oftentimes insurance companies won't cover counseling, and sometimes time, money, and patience run out before the proper treatment is found.

If you have lost someone to suicide, I sympathize with you. It hurts to think your loved one left this Earth that way. It also hurts to know that they left you with so much pain and many unanswered questions. I don't think people who commit suicide truly think about or comprehend how their actions will affect others. They simply can't see past their own pain. Suicide is a traumatic way to lose someone. I know you probably worry about what happened to your loved one after they took their own life. Everyone has his or her own beliefs on this subject. Traditional religion may disagree with me; however, it is my belief that our loved ones are still greeted with love when they pass. Just like everyone else. They will have to do a life review once they cross over. Everyone has one. They have to look at how their actions affected others. It is my belief that everyone has to do this when they die. In addition to the life review, they also receive gentle and loving healing…just as someone who had any other illness does. The soul becomes healed once again. If you are feeling guilt over the loss of a loved one who died by suicide because perhaps you believe you didn't see the signs, please let that guilt go. No amount of guilt will bring your loved one back. Punishing yourself will not alter the outcome. Your loved one doesn't want you to continue torturing yourself, either. Guilt isn't going to change one thing. Even if your loved one blamed you for their suicide in a note they left, that is the illness talking. People with mental illness have altered perceptions of reality. Once on the other side, they see the truth once more.

Guilt only puts us in a mental prison. It is a very low vibrational emotion, and it's really just another form of fear. I believe that all of our emotions in the end boil down to either love or fear. What are you afraid of? Are you afraid that your loved one is mad at you? Are you afraid that they suffered during their death? Are you afraid that they are in Hell suffering now? Let me just clear up some of that fear for you. Even if a loved one's death is violent, they don't remember the pain and suffering once they have crossed over. At least they don't suffer from it. Suffering is only a human condition that we experience here, and boy don't we love to experience it! Also, only love exists on the other side. If your loved one was mad at you when they died, they no longer feel that. Anger is a negative human emotion. They only feel love for you on the other side. On the other side, we are able to see the bigger picture in life. We see and understand why certain things have to happen to us. It's almost like a play where we all have our roles. We act out different scenarios to experience life lessons. We actually agreed to come here together and work through situations. Our tiny little human brain just isn't able to comprehend this. I'm not insulting you. I have a tiny little human brain too, and it's hard to imagine that we chose to suffer. The truth is that we did.

As for the Hell issue, I will again ruffle some feathers, but I don't believe in the Hell that we are taught about through religion. If you disagree with me, that is perfectly fine. We all have to choose our own beliefs in life. It is my belief after studying a lot of history, that what we are taught in religion is just another form of control. Why do you think there are so many different religions out there? I'm not downplaying your faith, either. I respect anyone who belongs to a religion. It's just not for me. I believe that a forgiving and loving God does exactly that. We are loved and healed when we get to the other side. I do think that you have to come back and try again when you take your own life, but isn't that the definition of grace? Forgiving and allowing someone to fix their mistakes. That's also the real definition of karma. The actions that we take in this lifetime determine what happens in the next. We have to come back to learn what we didn't learn the first time. It's sort of like repeating a grade in school.

I know that many people do not believe in past lives or reincarnation. Again, I completely understand if you don't. I do believe in them. There are so many children who talk about having been someone else, and they can describe that person and their life. Researchers are then able to find information about the person the child claims to have been. It matches, and there is no way that a child of 4 or 5 could have known that kind of information. If you would like to learn more about this, Dr. Brian Weiss is a good source. I believe that this is how we learn, and that's exactly why we came here to this Earth school. We came to learn as much as we could.

One of the biggest lessons we learn when we come here is about forgiveness. I forgave my ex, and let me tell you it wasn't easy. It took a lot for me to do this with my human heart. If I can forgive in my human existence, don't you think a much higher vibrational being, like God, the Divine, or whatever you call your higher power, is able to forgive that much easier? Of course, They can. What I have learned through careful studying and interviewing people who have had near death experiences is that once our loved ones transition to the other side, they don't worry about things like guilt, shame, or blame. All they feel is the genuine love you had for them, and that is what you need to focus on too.

If you are having trouble letting go of guilt, which is normal, then I have some tools that can help you work through it. The first step is to acknowledge your feelings of guilt. Guilt is a normal part of the grief process, and what you are going through is something that happens to a lot of people. Next, I want you to think about why you feel guilty. What do your thoughts keep telling you? What is it that is making you experience these intense feelings of guilt?

After you have acknowledged your guilt and examined why you are feeling it, I want you to think about whether those feelings are rational or not. For example, I thought I didn't do enough to help my mom fight this cancer. I needed to determine whether I really hadn't done enough or not. When I journaled and wrote down all the things I had done to help her, the list kept growing and growing. When I looked at my list, I realized that thinking I didn't do enough was completely irrational. My proof was in everything that I had written down. I saw with my own eyes that I had indeed done a great deal to help her. My brain was simply telling me that I hadn't. I saw a quote posted by Dr. Angela Pobanz on Instagram. I thought it was worth mentioning here. It said, "Just because you feel guilty doesn't mean you are guilty." That is such a true statement.

Humans are conditioned to feel guilt from a young age because it was a tool our parents and educators used to teach us the difference between right and wrong. As adults, guilt can consume our lives if we allow it. Sometimes people even use it as a weapon to control us. That is why we are so prone to feelings of guilt when tragedy strikes. Our brains automatically want to assume that we did something wrong or that we could have prevented it. The truth is that we could not. Let's imagine that you did your journaling, and you still think there were more things you could have done to help your loved one. Or maybe you had a fight with them right before they died. These things do happen. What would you do if this occurred when they were still alive? You would probably apologize…correct? Unless you are a mean, bullheaded, stubborn ass, you would try to make it right. I'm kidding…you're not an ass. You can still make it right, though. Write an apology letter to your loved one and let them know how sorry you are or how much you love them. I believe they can still hear us, and they will definitely feel the love you have for them. Plus, you will be able to let go of the guilt more easily if you work through it with your apology letter. After you apologize to your loved one, you need to forgive yourself. We're human. We make lots and lots of mistakes. In fact, we're supposed to make mistakes. That is the number one way we learn. It was your first attempt at learning, and you didn't quite get it right. Give yourself a break. What did you learn from this experience? That is all we need to take away from it. The guilt and shame need to stay behind. Now that you know better, you will do better in the future.

Another tool that I really like using is EFT or emotional freedom technique. This is commonly referred to as tapping. EFT is an alternative treatment for physical pain and emotional distress. It's also referred to as psychological acupressure. It is believed that this treatment can assist in managing troubling thoughts or emotions. So, how does it work? The first thing you do is think of the emotion that is bothering you, in this case, guilt. On a scale of 0-10, how bothered are you by guilt? 0 means you are not bothered at all, and 10 means you are extremely bothered by guilt…like it's controlling your life and consuming your thoughts. Create a statement that best describes your emotion.

An example for me would be, "I am feeling guilty that I did not do enough to save my mom's life." Next, create a follow-up statement that uses self-acceptance. I would use something like this: "Although I believe I didn't do enough to help save my mom from cancer, I loved her and did everything humanly possible to help her. I did enough to help her." Then you will tap repeatedly on different points of your body while repeating these statements. The most common areas to tap are usually the top of the head, the side of the eye, under the eye, under the nose, on the chin, and under the arm.

You can also do a search on YouTube for EFT tappings on guilt if you prefer to have someone else help guide you through this activity. Brad Yates is a great person to follow, but there are a lot of amazing professionals on YouTube who teach EFT. When you finish the tapping, measure how you are feeling again. On a scale of 0-10, how bothered are you by guilt now? Keep tapping until you are at a 0 or a 1 on the scale.

Guided meditations are another great tool to help you release those stored emotions. You can search YouTube for a guided meditation for releasing guilt. Find one that you like. One thing I would like to point out is that people assume that you're going to love every meditation you come across.

The truth is that not every meditation may work for you. If you don't like a person's voice or the music is irritating, it may be harder for you to relax. You might not want to do a guided meditation if Janice from Friends were leading it, you know what I mean? If you like my voice, I have a guided meditation on my YouTube channel for releasing negative emotions. How do you know if you like my voice, you ask? Go listen to my podcast, "Awaken Your Inner Awesomeness." You can find a sample there (wink). Don't you just love perfectly placed product promotion? I digress. In the same way that you measured the intensity of your guilt for EFT, measure it before you meditate. When you are done, take another measurement of the intensity of your emotion. Keep doing the guided meditation (do it once a day) until you feel that those emotions are not as intense. Another reason that I really like guided meditations is that they are relaxing and have positive physiological effects on the body. You know, things like lowering your blood pressure and cortisol levels. As a woman in her 40's, all I hear about right now is how important it is to lower cortisol levels. It stresses me out and raises my cortisol levels. I'm going to go do a meditation. I'll be right back.

Biofield tuning, Reiki, and other forms of energy healing are also extremely helpful in healing stored emotions. You can try out some of the different types of energy healing. There are several practitioners who put energy healing videos on YouTube. Sound healing is also a great way to release stored emotions. There are energy healers who have videos using singing bowls or tuning forks on various social media platforms. If you find that they help you at all, you can purchase a package of healing sessions with a professional energy healer. I did a few Biofield tuning sessions after my mom died. I have a good friend who is a practitioner. I hadn't realized how much old stored emotion I had. It was very relaxing, but at one point, I broke down sobbing.

There was such a release of emotion. I felt so much better after I had the session. I felt like I had released years of negative energy that had been stored in my body. We don't even realize just how much negative emotion we hold onto. It's like using a pressure cooker and releasing the steam. If you don't release it, the cooker will explode. It's so important for your physical, emotional, and spiritual well-being to release those stored emotions every so often.

Another thing that I like to do when trying to release guilt, is to have a conversation with the person that I need forgiveness from. You may be saying to yourself, "Melissa, are you completely insane? The person I need to have a conversation with is gone. They aren't here anymore. I can't talk to them." Well, for your information, I am insane. Just kidding. No one has committed me yet. I am not crazy, and you can talk to your loved one who is crossed over.

I mentioned this earlier, but if you feel like you need to ask for forgiveness, then do it. You can speak directly to your loved one. You don't need a medium to do that. Furthermore, you don't even have to say anything out loud because they can hear your thoughts. In the words of the John Mayer song, "Say what you need to say." It will make you feel better to speak your truth. I know that your loved one isn't holding a grudge, but forgiveness is for you anyway. It may ease your guilt to ask them for forgiveness or just to tell them how you feel. Our loved ones actually want to help us heal, and they are still around us lovingly guiding us. I mentioned earlier that writing a letter to your loved one helps to release negative emotions. When we put our thoughts down on paper, they no longer take up space in our minds. It helps us to process our emotions if we can verbalize or even write about what we are feeling.

I know that it can be difficult to break negative cycles of thought, but you need to stop blaming yourself for what you think you did or didn't do. Instead, honor the love that you had for the person you lost. Only love is real, anyway. Beating yourself up will only add to your pain. Buddha once said, "Pain is inevitable. Suffering is optional." It's true. We are the cause of our own suffering 99.9% of the time. Your loved ones do not want to see you hurting. They want you to live a beautiful, abundant, and joy-filled life. When those negative thoughts about guilt come up, and they will, acknowledge them and then let them go. They aren't serving your highest good. Instead, replace those thoughts with something like this…"I loved (fill in the name of your loved one) very much. I am grateful for the time, the love, and the memories we shared." Then use one of the tools I mentioned above to help you release that guilt.

Remember this one thing. When it is our time to go, nothing can keep it from happening. This is a part of the plan that we had for our lives when we came into this world. I say this only to bring you some comfort in knowing that you did your best. You couldn't have prevented your loved one's death, and you did enough. Your loved one knows that too, and they want you to keep going. They want you to remember the good memories and know that there are so many more amazing and beautiful memories yet for you to make. You don't have to have all the answers right now. Just take a deep breath and take it one day at a time, one step at a time, one moment at a time. Tell yourself the following things every day. I can let go of my past. I release shame. I release guilt. Now, let those things go. It will get easier gradually. Just remember to breathe, keep your chin up, and try to find a little inner peace. You deserve to be at peace, and you deserve to find joy again.

Here is a prayer to Archangel Gabriel for releasing guilt and shame:

Dear Archangel Gabriel,

I humbly ask you to help me release all of this guilt and shame that I am feeling right now. When my loved one died, it left me feeling helpless. I now know that I could not have prevented my loved one's passing. Please assist me in releasing the pain of this loss. Allow me to remember the beautiful memories that we shared instead of the pain of my loss. Thank you for helping me heal.

Amen

CHAPTER 5

ANGER: I'M MAD AT THE WHOLE DAMN WORLD

Anger is the next stage of grief, and it can be quite tough to work through, especially if you feel that your loved one suffered or had a traumatic death, or if your loved one died very young. This stage may also be extremely intense for you if you feel that your loved one's death was out of your control. I know that I personally struggled immensely with this emotion. I felt so much anger when my mom first died, especially the first few weeks after she passed. I was angry at the whole world. If I am being completely honest, though, I was angry before she even died. I was upset and felt hopeless with the medical system at large. I was furious at her doctors for giving her too much chemo when her body clearly couldn't handle it. I was livid that when I told them she had one kidney that didn't function normally and asked if it was more dangerous for her to get chemo, they didn't seem concerned. I just couldn't believe that they weren't concerned. I was frightened for her after everything I had read about the effects of chemo on the body. As a society, we tend to trust anyone in a white coat. Unfortunately, we shouldn't trust someone just because they are a physician. Just like anything else, that trust has to be earned. Of course, there are wonderful physicians out there, and there are also terrible physicians. It is just like any other profession. Doctors should listen to your concerns, so if you have one who doesn't, I suggest you find a different doctor.

My anger kept growing because I did a lot of research about how to fight cancer, and a lot of what they were doing with treatment was the opposite of what I was reading should be done. I have interviewed medical professionals on my podcast. Many of them talk about how they do not get training on nutrition or natural healing agents. They get training in medicine. I know that I am not a medical professional, but some of it is just common sense…like making sure that your immune system is supported when you are about to give a patient something that will completely destroy it. I was perplexed and incensed that they weren't concerned about her weight loss or actively trying to build her weight back up again. Yes, they did have her do a consultation with a dietitian. She told her to drink protein shakes. There are two major issues with this solution. Many protein shakes are filled with sugar, and sugar feeds cancer. Also, drinking shakes didn't work very well when my mom couldn't swallow, or when everything tasted like metal to her. It was all we could do to get her to drink even one shake. In fact, my daughter and niece still laugh about the first time she opened one of those shakes. She smelled it, made a bad face, and said, "This smells like protein." Not sure what fragrance protein has, but she could definitely detect it.

Can I just take a moment to say that our treatment of cancer is horrendous. We're giving patients substances that kill their immune system, cause their hair to fall out, and everything tastes like heavy metals to them. We're pumping them full of poison. Why is this even a thing? I'm so perplexed by the use of chemo. I need someone to make it make sense to me. I mentioned above that sugar feeds cancer. This Is fairly common knowledge. Astonishingly enough, only one person ever told my mom that she should be avoiding sugar, and that was her home healthcare nurse. Her oncologists never told her to change her diet at all. I know from the research that I've done that diet plays a huge role in the treatment of cancer. The staff at her oncology office never told her to avoid sugar or to eat foods that were high in antioxidants or anti-inflammatory agents. Their treatment for everything was surgery, chemo, and radiation. My mom did not respond well to any of those treatments.

I was filled with rage the last time she went into the hospital. She got a massive infection, which we later learned that chemo causes...surprise surprise. I didn't realize that the chemo causes infection until an ICU doctor told me that. It would have been nice to know that we should be watching for infection. I had no clue. I just knew that something was horribly wrong with her after her last chemo treatment. I was livid at the hospital for taking a week to decide how to treat her when she was lying in bed in pain. It just felt like they couldn't be bothered by her. I know they were probably busy, but when it's your loved one, you want action. You don't want them to suffer.

She had often gone without eating all day because they were unsure whether they would perform a procedure on her to drain the infection. We didn't realize how close to death she actually was. I watched a heart-wrenching video the other day on TikTok. It was a hospice nurse who was talking about her experience with a family she had recently worked with. She said that their loved one was actively dying and no one had made the family aware of what was happening. They just told the family to put their loved one on hospice to help manage pain. The family was still actively trying to save their loved one by giving her treatments. That is what happened to us too. No one ever said this is what is going to happen. No one sat us down and said this is what's happening to her body, and this is what to expect. We were stunned when things turned out the way they did. This nurse said she was so angry at the medical professionals who failed this family. They should have been made aware of what was happening. I totally agree with her. I know that no one wants to be the bearer of bad news, but it is so helpful to be prepared for what is to come.

The worst part for me, and something that only fueled my anger even more, is that when I would express how I felt, some of my family and friends would try to tell me that my anger was irrational. They would say things like, "The medical professionals did all they could. She had the best doctors out there. There is no way what you are doing can save her. Don't blame the doctors." They made me feel as though I was wrong for feeling what I did. I know they meant well, but they were basically making me feel as though my emotions were silly and nonsensical. Don't ever try to tell a person what they should or shouldn't feel. My emotions were and are valid. While I appreciate the medical community as a whole, there were definitely things they did wrong. In fact, the more I learn about natural medicine and how our body heals, the more I realize that Western medicine sometimes does more harm than good. It blows my mind that chemo and radiation are still our best options for cancer treatment. It's barbaric. The treatment for cancer is much worse than the cancer itself.

Bedside manners go a long way too when you are dealing with a serious illness. We were often treated as though my mom were cattle. Sometimes you feel like you become a nameless, faceless being. Her appointments took all day. She had a blood test when she first came in for her appointment, and she would then wait an hour or two for her appointment (she waited in uncomfortable lobby chairs no less); then she would find out if she could get treatment. That would take a few more hours. How much precious time did we waste sitting in a doctor's office? She was just another patient to them. She was just another "take a number and go have a seat" to them. What is worse is that she knew it too. She would often make comments to me that they didn't care about her. That became especially apparent in the end stages of her life. It hurt my heart that she felt that way. She wasn't wrong. Once she went into the hospital the last two times, we never heard from her oncologist again. It's like she was never his patient.

At first, her medical team built her up and told her that she had a good chance of fighting this disease. They found it early, and it was in the head, not the tail of the pancreas. After a modified Whipple surgery and many rounds of chemo, they declared her cancer-free and done with chemo. She rang the bell and thanked everyone at the doctor's office for their care. She could wait a few months to have another scan. We were so happy. We really thought she was going to survive. We thought she had beat the odds. We were almost done with this nightmare. We celebrated and thanked God that this was going to be over soon. We literally went out and celebrated because we thought the worst was over. It was as if, with a switch of a button, our world suddenly and cataclysmically shifted.

That follow-up scan a few months later was the beginning of the end for us. They found more cancer. At first, they said it was small, and they thought they could remove it with mere laparoscopic surgery. On the day of her surgery, they went in, saw that the cancer was free-floating, and couldn't get it, so they decided to do nothing.

I won't soon forget the call from my brother. He was crying and saying that it wasn't good. I remember thinking, "But they said it was small." Once she came home from the hospital, we waited for several weeks until they had a plan for her. They waited too long to decide what to do. In that time of waiting, I truly believe my mom's mindset deteriorated to a lethal level. It felt like God played a cruel joke on us. First, we think she is going to survive, and we are celebrating, and just months later, we are grasping for hope. I can't think of anything more cruel.

I don't know when some medical professionals lose their empathy; I suppose you have to in order to be able to function in that setting. It must be heart-wrenching to see death and dying every day. What I do know is that a little empathy goes a long way, especially when you are watching your loved one die before your very eyes. This may be just a patient to you, but this was my mom. This was my world. This is someone's cherished loved one. I will never forget when she was in the hospital for the last time. We were worried about what was happening to her, and no one was really telling us what was going on. Her hands and feet were swelling up. I was with her alone in her room. Because of COVID, we couldn't have more than one visitor a day. A doctor on call came in and bluntly told us that she was worried about my mom because she probably had 6 months to live. That was it. The words were spoken. It was at that moment that my world crashed. That was the first time anyone had given us any sort of time frame, and she just blurted it out so coldly. I watched my mom's face at first as it filled with fear, and then I held her while she began sobbing. Meanwhile, I secretly plotted my revenge on that doctor in my head. How cruel can some people be? Why would she just announce that my mom had 6 months to live so casually as if it wasn't totally devastating news? Why didn't someone before her have a conversation with us to help us understand what was happening? I felt sick and extremely scared. The worst part was that I was alone. I had to tell my siblings what that doctor said. For the first time on this journey, I felt completely hopeless. My mom actually ended up passing away just a few days later. Don't tell me that when someone loses their will to fight, it doesn't change outcomes.

I was frustrated and annoyed at the world at large for everything, but especially COVID. COVID prevented us from going to visit her more than one person at a time. I often had to make difficult decisions about her in the hospital by myself, and so did my siblings. COVID prevented her from seeing two of her sisters and her mom before she died. I was generally just pissed off that my mom was taken from me at 69 years old, especially when I would see people whose moms lived to be 98. It wasn't fair. None of this was fair. I'll be honest. I still struggle each and every single day with anger. It comes to me in waves. I still have a difficult time understanding why she had to go through this. I still struggle to grasp the finality of it all. It still feels like I'm walking through a daydream, hoping that one day this nightmare will end.

After she died, and we had the gut-wrenching task of planning her funeral, we were sitting with the funeral director trying to figure out what we were going to do. We decided to hold the funeral at the church that my brother and I used to attend. My mom helped me lead the music program for vacation bible school for several years there. In fact, she volunteered with me for many things, like working the free dinners the church had or helping with the after-school homework program. We were no longer members there because there was a falling out with the pastor of the church. We liked him and disagreed with what happened, so we stopped going. The new pastor said we could have the funeral there, but we would need to let her perform some part of the ceremony and would have to pay her. This didn't seem unreasonable to us. My mom already had a wonderful minister in mind to perform her service, but we agreed that this minister could say a closing prayer, and we would pay two ministers.

It seemed like everything was in order, so we finished our planning and drove home. On the way home, the funeral director called. I was on the phone with my dad at the time letting him know what the plans were. The funeral director said that the church had called back and stated that we wouldn't be able to hold the service there after all. They told him to tell us they forgot that they had booked something else, but he said they mentioned something about the lack of tithing. So, at a point in our lives where we were at our lowest, we felt like we got punched in the gut yet again. I was furious. My mom was never a member of that church, but she volunteered for them with VBS and served food for the free dinners they held there for people in need. My mom always gave of her time so freely, and now it felt like this church was saying that she wasn't good enough for them. I was glad that I was no longer a member. That church affirmed for me in that moment why I dislike organized religion. I will say that my sister's church stepped up, and her priest was the kindest human. He let us use their church and let us live stream the service. He just kept asking us how he could help us and kept saying how wonderful he thought my mom was.

I could not wrap my head around why our former church treated us so badly. It was hard for me to believe that it was all over a lack of money, but they do say that money makes the world go around. All I know is that it made me sick to my stomach. It felt like my mom had been disrespected. Her memory seemed tarnished all because this church chose money over people.

When the day of my mom's wake came, we went in to view her. I already had knots in my stomach. I always hate going in to view a body. You never know how someone will look or how it will make you feel when you see the person. Visitations make me anxious as it is. Now, I was here for my mom. It seemed surreal.

When we went in, we were all shocked by how bad my mom looked. Yes, she had been sick, but it had more to do with the fact that the way they did her makeup and painted her nails was not at all my mom's style. I understand that this can happen if funeral homes are relying on pictures to recreate the look of a loved one, but my mom had actually worked at this funeral home. After she retired, she handled donations and worked visitations for them. The people who worked with her knew her. They saw her frequently. She had on a weird shade of orange lipstick. It was as if in unison, everyone saw it and had a panicked look on their faces. I wanted to wipe it off of her and apply a different shade, but it was too late. Family came in right behind us. We didn't have any personal time alone with her, so I was unable to change her lipstick. Even that felt helpless for me. Every time I looked at her, I could hear her griping about that lipstick. She was probably really telling us off from the other side. In the swirl of events that took place after her death, I was too busy to really sit with my grief.

Once things settled down, and the reality of her absence started to sink in, a million questions played on a loop in my head. Why is my mom gone? Why do I have to live the rest of my life without her? Who will I call now when I need someone? Who will I text when I have good news? There are still days when I ask myself these questions. The truth is that I will never really get the answers, at least not in this lifetime. Questioning why will not bring my mom back. Torturing that ignorant doctor will not bring her back. Cursing a minister will not bring her back. Leaving a bad review for a funeral home will not bring her back. Nothing will bring her back. I did not leave a bad review for that funeral home, by the way, because they were absolutely amazing with everything else…just not the orange lipstick. So, how do you get through the anger? How do you let go of all the frustration and resentment that you feel?

It is so important that you work through your anger. Carrying it around with you will only make your suffering worse. The first and most important thing to understand is that everything you are feeling is valid. You need to honor your emotions. They came up for a reason. Acknowledge that you are angry. If people try to make you feel like your feelings aren't valid, ignore them. They are wrong and are idiots. I might still be a little angry. Anyway, you have to get it out. I talked to the Universe directly when I expressed my emotions. I said out loud how mad I was. I even told God that I was mad at Him. People think that it isn't OK to question God, or the Universe, or whatever you call your higher power. Why isn't it OK? There is this unspoken belief that we are not allowed to be mad at God or our higher power, that it is somehow blasphemous. I don't believe that at all. I think, if anything, God wants us to talk to Him. Doesn't it say to cast all of your cares on Him? I think that means not only your burdens, but your complaints too. The only way to truly process and get out your emotions is to express them. I don't think God minds. If anything, we can ask for help in letting the anger go. We can also ask for help understanding what we are going through. Additionally, our higher power can provide us with some guidance.

I went to a grief group with my sister after my mom died. There was a person in that group who was so angry, but she didn't feel like she had the right to be angry. She didn't know how to work through her anger. Sometimes, just understanding that you are not alone is enough to help you start to heal. Sometimes you just need someone to tell you that it is OK to be pissed off. Guess what, I'm telling you that it's normal and OK for you to be mad at the world when you are going through grief. What is not OK is to stay in that place for a long time or to take it out on someone else. Being bitter isn't going to make you feel better. Getting revenge is not going to help you feel better. Yes, the plotting of it may, but if you actually carry it out, you will feel terrible about it eventually. You have to get your anger out so that you can work through it and move to the other side of it. Beautiful things await us when we work through our pain.

Sometimes when we question, we do get answers. Though I didn't get the specific answers to the questions I asked, what I did get was reassurance. I received signs from my mom. God brought some amazing people into my life and used them to bring me signs from my mom. Her favorite song was You are my Sunshine. She would teach every child she knew that song. My best friend's mom bought my sister and I a blanket with the lyrics to that song on it. She had no idea the song was a favorite of my mom's. She bought it because it said "To my daughter." She wanted to get us something thoughtful. She had no idea how thoughtful it actually was. I believe that the blanket was a message straight from my mom, and it came just a few days after her passing. As I am in the process of writing this book, she also came through with some very strong signs. I was on the phone with my daughter Ally, when the lights went out. I thought that perhaps our power had gone out, but the television was still on. I walked over to inspect the lights, and I found the light switch was turned in the off position. That happened to me twice in one week. In order for the lights to turn off, someone has to press down on the switch and apply pressure to it. My daughter and I were both stunned. She let us know and still lets us know that she is doing so well and that she is still very much with us. She feels so much better, and she is no longer in pain. That is enough for me to stop having a pity party for myself and realize that I wouldn't want my mom back even if I could have her back. Why? That would be selfish of me. I don't want to see her in pain anymore. I sometimes believe that Earth is the real Hell. This is where we came to learn and grow, and it isn't easy. Would I want to drag her back here just so I could feel better? No, I wouldn't. She did her time here. She earned her celebration and graduation to the other side.

Although I have tried to make peace with her passing, I am human, and I still get angry sometimes. I was very angry at my ex when he took his own life. I thought it was an extremely selfish thing to do. I was furious that he could hurt our children so much. I was mad that he left me here to tell our children what he did. I was pissed that he left such a big mess for me to clean up. I didn't know how I was supposed to afford college for my kids now that I had to do it alone. I was angry and worried that my kids would never recover from this emotionally. How were they supposed to get over his death? How could he do this to them? There are days when I still don't understand what he did. I still get mad. I just want life to be a little easier for my kids.

When I do get angry, I acknowledge my anger. I tell myself that this anger is really just pain. It's the confusion of not understanding why things had to happen the way that they did. It is the lack of control that I had over my mom's death. It's the guilt that I didn't do all the things I should have. It's all the things wrapped up into this one strong emotion. Those emotions were really just a side effect of the love I had for my mom spilling out in different ways. I believe strongly that we choose our time of birth and our time of death before we ever come here. I don't think there is anything that you can do to prevent someone's death if it is their time to go. It is a person's destiny, whether we understand it or not. Every hair on our head has been accounted for, and there is a time and a place for every season. It has already been written. What I choose to focus on is the experience that my mom is having right now, instead of my pain. In fact, when my mom first passed, I called the minister that she was friends with to let him know that she had died. He was going to perform at her funeral. His words to me were, "Oh Melissa, what she must be seeing right now." It still brings tears to my eyes thinking about what he said. Although I was in immense pain, his words brought me comfort somehow. We often can't see past our own pain to realize how wonderful it will be for our loved ones when they cross over to the other side. What our loved ones experience when they transition is a joyous reunion in a place that is even more beautiful than we could ever imagine. They feel like they stepped out of clothes that no longer fit. They are no longer burdened by bodies that betrayed them. They get to do all the things that they love, and they can still come visit us anytime they wish.

I know you are grieving for what you are experiencing, and I am not trying to diminish the validity of your pain. However, if you shift your focus a little, you will realize that we should be happy for our loved ones. They're not sad, miserable, or hurting. We're the ones who suffer. Remember that suffering is a human thing. They are enjoying the reward that they so richly deserved for a life well lived. Even if you think your loved one didn't live their life honorably, remember this. We are all on our own journeys and paths in life. We had to learn specific lessons when we came here.

Perhaps your loved ones' lesson involved living in a way that you didn't approve of. It isn't our place to judge. It's simply our place to love them where they are. When I find myself going to that dark place, and I still sometimes do, I try to remember to give thanks for the beautiful memories I shared with my mom. I remember all the things about her that made me proud that she was my mom. It's ok to feel angry. Try not to stay in that space for too long. Talk to your loved one. They can still hear you. Tell them how you feel. They want to help you heal.

I learned about a really cool exercise in the grief group I attended. They said to write yourself a letter from the viewpoint of your loved one. What would he or she say to you if they were still here? If they had 5 minutes to leave heaven and come talk to you, what would they say to you? Do you really think they would say anything negative? No, they wouldn't. They wouldn't want to waste the precious time they had with you. They would probably tell you how much they love and miss you. They might tell you how proud they are of you. They would probably say that they are still with you. They wouldn't spend any of that time saying things that didn't really matter. Our souls in their natural state are just pure love. Your loved one would want to shower you with so much love and affection.

Something that I find extremely comforting is that our loved ones still want to help us and show us they are still around. Ask for signs from your loved one. Ask for specific signs. You may even feel their presence. My mom likes to use music to show us that she is still here. We'll talk more about signs in a future chapter. For now, have grace with yourself. This is not an easy journey. Don't beat yourself up when you feel angry.

Instead, ask yourself these questions. What is this really about? Why am I so angry? Will my anger bring back my loved one? How is this anger helping me? In understanding our anger, we can more easily process it. Is there anything you can do to change what happened? The answer is most likely no. A lack of control can often make us feel angry or afraid. That's a normal reaction. It's important to find a healthy outlet for your anger. You need to express it, so you can release it.

Sometimes our anger is due to the way that we treated a loved one before they passed. In that same grief group session, a woman was angry at herself because she was mad at her loved one before he died. He wasn't making good life choices, and she hung up on him the last time she spoke to him.

That loved one died of an overdose just a few days later. If you are experiencing anything similar to this, you need to forgive yourself and the person who passed. We all have free will in life. You can't control anyone or force anyone to get help who isn't ready. You can't drag people to the doctor or make them eat right. Lack of control is probably one of the biggest contributors to feelings of frustration and anger. Let it go. Forgiveness is more about you than the other person.

It's about deciding that you're going to let go of the heavy burden that your anger is causing you. You are human, and you're going to make mistakes. Sometimes our emotions get the best of us, and we lash out at our loved ones. Being angry and resentful at someone is like drinking poison and expecting the other person to die. You are really only hurting yourself. You need to forgive and let go. There is a wonderful website called Radical Forgiveness. They have online worksheets where you can walk through what happened in a way that allows you to see the lesson in the situation, so you can let go of the anger, hurt, resentment, or any other negative emotion that might be torturing you. You really are keeping yourself held hostage in a mental prison when you hold onto anger.

How can you release this anger that you are feeling? How do you let it go? I'm going to share with you some tips for working through anger. If you do the work, you can let go of your anger and start to feel better again, and I know you want to feel better. The first tip is to break your stuff. You read that right. I'm serious. You can break something (safely). Just grab whatever old, ugly, and fragile thing you can find around your house. Aim, throw, smash, and you will feel better. They even have smashing rooms now. You can go and release your anger by breaking things in a controlled environment. You will release that anger, and no one will get hurt. Plus, it could be a fun girls' or guys' night out. Another thing you can do is to scream. Scream out whatever words come to you. This could be a long string of obscenities. One thing I would suggest is to do this alone or when you are with someone who doesn't mind. Never scream at someone because that is abusive. Scream out loud and say what you need to say, but again, don't ever direct this at someone. You don't want to cause harm to anyone else. You could even scream into a pillow. Find a place where you feel comfortable and let it out. That brings me to the third tip, which is to sing it out. Singing is very powerful. I know plenty of songs that allow you to scream too, so you could always combine tips 2 and 3. Singing some good old-fashioned alternative rock is just what the doctor ordered. Go find a karaoke bar and have fun with it. I'm sure the audience will really enjoy your screaming... I mean singing.

If you are not into singing or screaming, you can get more physical. Dancing is a fun way to work through your emotions, and you would also be getting your exercise in. Speaking of exercising, this is another great way to work through anger. Movement releases endorphins into your body, which in turn elevates your mood. Who doesn't need a mood boost these days? One thing that I like to do is write. Journaling is a great way to get out what you are feeling. You can get yourself a cool looking journal...you know the ones with the inspirational sayings like "Good Vibes Only" or "Live, Laugh,

Love," or maybe one with a cat on it that says, "Hang in there, baby," or some other cheesy... I mean, cute stuff like that.

The important thing is to write whatever you are feeling or whatever comes to you. You never know, it could even turn into a book. If you don't like writing, you could talk into your phone memo recorder to get out what you need to say. The important thing is to say what you need to say. Speak your truth, so you can release those negative feelings.

If you are feeling creative, or you are an artistic person, you could create something beautiful from your anger. Painting, drawing, or sculpting is a great way to work through your pain. Most artists are so talented because they use their emotions to create. Turn that pain into a beautiful new project. Another idea that could help in your healing is to change your scenery for a bit. The new views will do you a world of good. After my mom died, my sister and I took a beach vacation. It was nice to be able to relax and enjoy some downtime in a beautiful environment. Nature is very healing. Being by water is also cleansing for the soul. A little weekend getaway might be just the thing you need to feel better.

When that anger rears its ugly head, tell yourself the following: I choose to release anger and reclaim my happiness. I choose to feel at peace now. I am releasing anger so that I may clear space for peace and love in my life. I am breathing deeply and letting go of this anger. The important thing is not to ignore your anger or pain. Ignoring it doesn't make it disappear. You have to process it. Be patient with yourself. You may have to process your anger multiple times because it's like peeling back the layers of an onion. You heal one layer and another emerges. There may be multiple layers. The good news is that it does get easier with each new layer. You will find that one day the anger no longer has control over you. You will begin to feel an inner peace once more. You deserve to live a joyful life. You can't do that if you are bitter or resentful. Take the time to work through your anger because life gets so much better when you do.

Here is a prayer to Archangels Muriel and Uriel (These are the archangels who assist in releasing difficult emotions):

Dear Archangels Muriel and Uriel,

I am so filled with anger and resentment, and I don't know what to do with these strong emotions. I ask you to help me process them so that I may release this anger and be filled with peace. Help me to understand what this anger is all about so that I may let go of the need to be angry or resentful. Fill me with an inner peace that I may feel better.

Amen

CHAPTER 6
BARGAINING: MAKING A DEAL WITH GOD

When our loved ones first die, it leaves us feeling so many different intense emotions. Among those is often desperation and despair. In fact, we may wish so fervently that our lives return to normalcy, that we even try to bargain with God or our higher power. Perhaps we think that we could convince the Universe that our loved one's life deserved to be spared. Maybe we hope that He will alleviate the pain we're feeling. There are so many ways that bargaining and desperation show up. Maybe you pleaded with God that if He spared your loved one, you would start going back to church or giving to the poor, or fill in the blank with whatever you thought might appease Him.

I know that when my mom was sick, I pleaded with the Universe all the time. I would say things like, "If you just let her live, I will do anything. I will teach everyone how to fight cancer. I will help as many people as possible." When that didn't work, I resorted to desperation. I begged. I researched everything I could about her health. I sought other healers and turned to holistic measures to try to restore her health. I asked God to bring people into our lives who could help us fight this awful disease. If the Universe could just grant me this one wish, I wouldn't ask for anything ever again. That's right, I actually promised the Universe that I wouldn't ask for another miracle ever again. Well, spoiler alert, the Universe didn't grant my wish. So, guess what? I'm still going to continue to ask for other miracles. I'm only kidding. The truth is that the Universe did answer my prayers, just not in the way that I expected. The Universe did send some amazing people into our lives to help us. So, although my prayers weren't answered the way I wanted them to be, they were still answered.

Perhaps you can understand my situation. Did you fall into that bargaining trap? Maybe you even asked the Universe to take you too because you just didn't want to live here on Earth without your loved one? I understand. No one wants to have to face a life without those they love. It can feel so lonely and empty. One thing that you need to consider, however, is that there is still so much life for you to experience. I count my blessings that I still have a lot of people to be here for. My children are the biggest reason why I still want to be here...for them. I don't want to miss any time with them.

That's the fascinating thing about this journey we call life. We can be in so much grief that we can't see the beautiful blessings all around us. I know that I have fallen into that rabbit hole a time or two. The problem with choosing to focus only on our grief is that it causes us to miss out on everything that is still here...things like cherished time with our loved ones or the amazing blessings that are waiting for us in the future.

It's tough because I understand wanting to isolate yourself. I know what it feels like to become a zombie. You want to dissociate so that you don't have to feel these horrible feelings anymore. If you aren't living in the present, then you don't have to face the harsh reality that your loved one isn't coming back. When my mom first died, I would catch myself thinking that she was just in the hospital. The reason she isn't here is that she's in the hospital getting better. My brain didn't want to deal with the truth. It caused me too much pain. The pain can be so intense that you don't want to go on. It feels like it would be better to just give up because this is too difficult. Maybe you simply want to stay in bed and throw the covers over your head because facing the world is unbearable. You would be well within your rights to do that. The problem is that life still goes on. You can't opt out. You are stuck here until it is your time to go. Do you really want to live out the rest of your life in isolation and numbness? Do you really just want to spend your life waiting to die? I know that you don't. You don't really want to miss out on the beautiful memories and experiences that are still to come. Thankfully, the Universe doesn't always grant our wishes. We would miss so much of this beautiful life, if it did.

When my mom first got sick, I searched frantically for answers. I wasn't content just begging for the Universe to heal my mom. I found myself wishing that the Universe could take me back to the month before my mom was diagnosed. If you just take me back in time, I will warn her sooner. She could get treatment sooner. Surely that would change the outcome. This type of thinking didn't start when my mom died. I remember when my cousin Jimmy died, I wished that I could turn back time to one day before the accident. I could have warned someone. We could have prevented him from leaving the house that night. Wouldn't it be nice if we could quantum leap and go around saving people like they do on the show? I mean, why can't we do that? We could have warned JFK or the astronauts on the Challenger. Why can't we save everyone? It's interesting the kind of intrusive thoughts you have after a great loss.

The harsh reality is that it is not our job to save anyone. If we believe in destiny, and I truly do, then we have to believe that all of this is preordained. Our birth and death dates have already been determined before we ever came here. Interference is not going to change that. Besides, no one would listen to you if you told them that you could predict the future. They would look at you like you are insane. My mom wouldn't have listened to me either. If she felt well, she would have scoffed at anyone asking her to visit a doctor. I have often thought that we should all be required to get bimonthly body scans, but that would be super expensive, and the insurance companies would certainly not pay for that. Plus, the extra radiation might cause cancer. It's a vicious cycle, isn't it? The difficult truth is that you can't wrap your loved ones up in bubble wrap. You can't protect them every single second of every day. Believe me, I want to do that to my kids.

Besides, my mom would've thought I was insane if I had told her she needed to go get a body scan. I can't change the past. Those thoughts that you should have done more are intrusive and don't really solve any problems. It does show you how the brain works. Our brains focus on negativity. It's a mechanism that at one time kept us safe. Now, however, it can be very harmful if we choose only to focus on negativity. If any of this resonates with you, then I want you to remember one thing. Bargaining is a very normal part of grief.

When my ex died, I remember thinking that maybe he staged his death, so he could disappear. If you knew him, It really does sound like something he might do. I think I held onto some hope that maybe he had faked his death. This possibility was better than the reality that he had taken his own life in such a horrific manner. My hope that he had somehow faked his death and skipped town was just another form of denial. I didn't want to face what I knew was true. If I faced the truth, I would have to accept that he had taken his own life on purpose and left his kids with all of this pain .

Bargaining and denial are very common after the death of a loved one. We don't want to have to face the reality that the worst possible scenario just happened. I mean, death is the worst thing, right? It's so final, and it is irreversible. Even if they came out tomorrow and said they had a cure for cancer, it wouldn't help my mom. It's too late. We'd rather try to convince our higher power to change the result than deal with the reality of what we're experiencing. At first, running from the truth feels better. It's more manageable to feel nothing than to experience the tough emotions we're feeling. As I stated in a previous chapter, it will only make things worse in the long run if you try to ignore your pain.

I mentioned in Chapter 5 that I believe our date of birth and death is predestined. I interviewed a guest on my podcast who had a near death experience. That guest stated that he learned that we have multiple possible exit points in our life. We have the ability to choose which exit point we wish to take once we get here. So, I suppose we have several possible death dates, which may explain why some people have near-death experiences where they are asked to choose whether to come back or go on. The point that I am trying to make is that even though we wish we could change someone's death, we can't. It isn't up to us. It's not our decision. Even if you had to make the painful choice to turn off life support for a loved one, you still didn't choose their destiny. It was planned before your loved one ever came here. So, if you are feeling guilty over having to make a decision like that, please let it go. We had to make the decision for my mom, and I know how difficult it can be. It is so much more humane to let our loved ones go than to allow them to suffer. I know you absolutely did the right thing. Just as we did the right thing for my mom.

I know a few people who have lost children, which I believe is the worst kind of pain you can feel. It isn't natural to outlive your child. I watched both my aunt and my grandma lose their children. My grandma lost my uncle when she was in her 70s, and you would have thought that he died a little boy...because he was her little boy. He would always be her little boy. I also know that she felt regret over his passing and wished that there were some way she could have saved her child. That is literally our job as parents. We are supposed to protect our kids. Losing them feels like the ultimate neglect of our duties. The problem with that is that you can't keep them locked up in a room, so they stay safe. You can't watch them twenty-four hours a day. We come into this world to experience life and to learn and grow. We are all on a unique journey. Sometimes that means you get hurt. While it doesn't seem fair, I go back to what I said earlier. Focus on the love you shared and the wonderful memories you made. We can't go back and save anyone. What has happened can't be changed, and we have to face it head on. Replaying the incidents that led to your loved one's passing will not bring them back. It will only torture you. The sooner you can begin to face the harsh reality that this is final, the sooner you can begin to heal and find peace.

What helped me and continues to help me get through this stage is to remember that my mom is in a much better place. If you could imagine your loved one surrounded by the most beautiful scenes in nature, smelling amazing flowers, playing with animals, feeling completely free of pain or suffering, would you want to bring them back here? We want to bring them back for selfish reasons. We want one last hug or one more "I love you." We want to be comforted. It's understandable because we made some beautiful memories and connections with our loved ones in this lifetime. The void in our lives is evident. Our hearts are breaking and longing for them. But if I am being honest with you, our loved ones wouldn't want to come back even if they could. They would have to give up all the beauty, unconditional love, and peace that they feel where they are now. This may seem like a silly example, but think about when you are in a comfy and warm bed and your alarm goes off. You don't want to get out of bed onto the cold floor. Your loved one doesn't want to leave their comfort either. This Earth is so heavy, and even some of us don't really want to be here. Would you want to pull them from a beautiful place to bring them back to this pit? I don't think so. Plus, they can still see us and hear us. They are always around us. They don't miss us because they never truly left us. They are simply at a different energetic level now. You are always one thought away from connecting to them. In a future chapter, we will talk about how you can connect to your loved ones by strengthening your intuitive abilities. When you learn how to get signs from them, it can bring you so much peace and comfort. In addition, you will get the physical proof you need to see that their love for you still very much exists.

If you find yourself saying "what if" or "if only," then you may be stuck in this bargaining stage. Bargaining is a defense mechanism that we utilize because we feel so helpless after a loss. We struggle to accept the reality of our loss, and we are frustrated by the lack of control over it. The first step in getting through this is to realize that you can not change anything that happened in the past. Even if now you see that things could have been handled differently, you can't change it. It's too late. You do not possess a time machine, and you can't go back and fix anything. You did the best you could with what you had. We can't predict what will happen with our loved ones from moment to moment. We wouldn't want to even if we could because we would always be in a constant state of fear and worry.

Once you acknowledge that you can't change your current situation, you need to let go of the ifs. To me, bargaining and guilt go hand in hand. We've already discussed that guilt doesn't do anything positive for you. That being said, sometimes those pesky thoughts will still haunt you. When they do, I want you to do the following. The first thing you should do is write down your thoughts. Write them down and really examine them. Now ask yourself the following questions. Are these thoughts rational? Are they logical? Are they helpful? The answer is most likely no. Now ask yourself this question. Am I currently in control of this? Again, your answer is probably no. Now I want you to redirect those thoughts. To do this, ask yourself this one question. What can I control? Come up with a list of everything in your life right now that you do have control over. Now look at your list. Is there anything you can be doing better? If so, make those changes in your life. Focus on that list instead of the list of all the things you can't control. You can change and improve things in your life for the better, but the only thing you can change is yourself and your present, not the past or anyone else.

It might be beneficial for you to do a tapping for releasing the need to control. Sometimes as children, we felt that a lot of decision-making was out of our control. We didn't really get choices in life. We were told what to do. I think that's why being out of control can feel so scary, especially if you had a chaotic home life. It's important to realize that we only have control over so much in life. We have control over our own actions and thoughts, and that is really about it. We can't control other people. We need to learn to let go of the need to feel that control. Once we do, life gets a lot easier. Remember that you are doing your best. We didn't receive a set of instructions when we came here. It would be so nice if we did. I received a 1,000-page instruction manual when I bought my car. We don't even get so much as one page when we are sent here. It's almost as if the Universe ships us out and says, "Good luck, sucker." Who knows how this is supposed to work? That is exactly the point. Do your best. Improve your life where you can, and let the rest go. Your loved one isn't sitting on the other side cursing you for not helping them more. You are the only one who is torturing yourself.

You have the key to end your own suffering. Let go of the guilt and the what ifs. Focus on the present. The rearview mirror is always small for a reason. We aren't supposed to spend our time looking backwards. You live your best life by living fully in the present. Focus on the blessing that you currently see around you. There are so many more coming. I promise!

CHAPTER 7

DEPRESSION: HOW DO I CRAWL OUT FROM THE DEEP DARK PIT

Depression is a stage of grief that I think is sometimes difficult to identify, at least it was for me. Depression causes a persistent feeling of sadness and loss of interest. It affects how you feel, think, and behave, and can lead to a variety of emotional and physical problems. A popular belief about depression is that it is easy to spot. Most people think depression looks like someone who can't get out of bed, stays in their pajamas all day, or someone who is sad every moment of every day. Yes, it can look like that, but this isn't always the case. Sometimes depression is subtle and sneaky. I realized that I was suffering from depression after my mom died, but I had no idea because it slowly took a hold of me, and it looked nothing like what I assumed traditional depression was.

I know what depression can look like. I witnessed depression first hand. My ex-husband suffered from depression. He had mood swings, and you could never predict what he might say or do. It was extremely frustrating and difficult to live with. Getting help for him was also complicated. He didn't like going to counseling, and he didn't like the way the medications they put him on made him feel. So, it was easier for him to do nothing to fight it. My son was also plagued by major depression during high school. I didn't realize that he was suffering from depression at the time. He was dealing with some trauma that occurred at the hands of his dad. It's also known that depression runs in families. I knew something was wrong with him, but I didn't know exactly what or why. I had difficulty getting him to turn in his school work because he just wasn't motivated, and I started noticing that he slept a lot. He would come home from school and go right to sleep. At first, I assumed this was because he was staying up too late at night playing video games. I simply believed that he was being a typical teenager. I didn't realize that he felt so hopeless and lost. He was also isolating himself. What I witnessed with my son was heart-wrenching. I knew that he was in a very dark place. Both my ex-husband and my son's symptoms were more obvious and severe. These were not the type of symptoms that I experienced when I was depressed at all. I did not spend all of my time sleeping after my mom died. I also didn't stop working, and I didn't feel unmotivated at work.

So, how did I know that I was experiencing depression? It was a sudden realization that hit me one day. I started noticing that it was the little things. I stopped doing the little things that I used to do to take care of myself. I stopped working out; in fact, it was extremely difficult to motivate myself to do any sort of exercise. I just chalked it up to being tired because of work. I quit practicing self-care. I stopped meditating and stopped my morning routine of listening to positive affirmations.

I was also weepy at certain times. It wasn't all the time. It would just come and go. Again, I just assumed that I was grieving, so that explained the sadness. What finally caused me to realize that I was depressed was the fact that I didn't want to be alone. Being alone seemed to trigger me. While my brother preferred to isolate and stay away from people, I needed to be around people. I needed my family. When I thought I might have to spend time alone, I would almost panic. I felt sad and lonely. I almost had a fear that if I wasn't around people, I would somehow never be around anyone again. That is how I knew that I was gripped by depression. I have always been a fairly independent person. I never had a problem spending time alone. As a matter of fact, I used to enjoy my alone time. A good day to me was going to get coffee, browsing through a few stores, and then coming home to watch something good on T.V. Now, I didn't want to do any of this. I was depressed, it had snuck up on me, and it held me tightly in its grip.

Depression may look very different for you. We are all unique beings, so our experiences will be unique as well. The important thing is to acknowledge when you aren't feeling your best and seek professional help when you need it. There is no shame in going to a counselor or attending grief groups. Both can be very helpful. Knowing that you are not alone and connecting with others who share experiences with grief can be extremely cathartic. Plus, you get to meet new people who may end up becoming allies for you. For me, individual grief counseling played a huge role in my healing. It was so comforting to have someone to vent my feelings to. My counselor was very supportive in whatever I was feeling, and she allowed me to speak freely and validated that my feelings were important. I didn't feel judged at all. She simply helped me work through those emotions in a healthy way. I always felt so much better after our sessions, and I didn't feel like I was burdening a friend or family member by talking about my grief. I know that my friends and family didn't see it as a burden when I shared how I was feeling. They were happy to allow me to talk about what I was going through, and it was helpful for them to also share their own stories of grief as well. It was for my own sense of peace that I chose to seek out counseling. While I knew that my family wanted to be there for me, I didn't want to always talk about how sad I was. I wanted my time with my family to be filled with happiness and joy. That is why I decided to seek help. Talking to a counselor also provided me with someone who could be objective and who could show me how to look at things from different perspectives.

The most important thing is to talk to someone. Whether you talk to a trusted friend, family member, or counselor, talking about what you are going through will help you immensely. Bottling up your emotions is unhealthy. Choosing not to talk about what you are feeling can cause the pain to become worse in the end. Those emotions do not disappear. They will simply be stored in your body. They have to come out eventually. Remember the sobbing wine party?

In my first book, I shared a story of a woman going through divorce. She was at a bachelorette party at a drag show. She sat and sobbed the entire time. If you don't deal with your emotions, you will be that woman or man sobbing at a drag show. Nobody wants that…especially the drag queens. It kind of puts a damper on the show. In the next few paragraphs, I will share with you some tips and tools that you can use on your own to help you move through your depression with more grace and ease. These tools can help you to feel better and help you move through your grief in a much more pleasant way. Seriously, the drag queens will thank you.

The first tip I have for you is not to withdraw from life. I know your initial instinct may be to isolate yourself. Maybe you simply don't feel like being around people. Perhaps you feel like you don't have the energy to go out. I understand that. It is perfectly normal to feel that way. The problem is that we are extremely communicative beings, and we need that human connection in our lives. You may feel like you're not good company, or you may feel like a zombie when you are around others, but I promise you that it does help to continue connecting to people. Sometimes at first, you may have to fake it until you make it. Force yourself to stay connected. I have known people who chose to withdraw when they started to feel depressed. This will not help your depression at all. It will only make it worse. You will sink deeper into isolation, and that really only leads to more depression. It's a vicious cycle, really. If you have family or friends that you can lean on, please reach out to them. I had a friend who didn't contact me after my mom died because she didn't want to burden me with her problems. She felt like I was already going through enough. I didn't need to hear about her struggles. When we finally got together, and she told me what was going on with her, it actually made me feel better. We both realized that talking about her problems helped both of us. It felt so comforting for me to know that I wasn't the only one struggling, and I enjoyed helping her work through her problems. It also took the attention away from my own struggles for a bit.

Sometimes just knowing you are not alone can be a huge relief and help you to breathe easier.

The second tip I have for you is to be more active. This one was especially difficult for me. I had to force myself to get off the couch and go for walks when I was feeling sad. All I really wanted to do was cuddle up with a warm blanket and watch trash TV, and believe me I had a lot of shows to choose from. I understand how you feel, and it's fine to do this once in a while, but you don't want to waste your life away. Sure, sitting on the couch with a gallon of ice cream and a heated blanket is nice, but it isn't really helping you process your grief. You need to get back out there. Getting back out into the world will show you that there are still so many things going on. Going for walks helped me to clear my head and get more grounded. Getting out in nature is a great way to balance your emotions. It also made me feel better, too. Experts say we need time in the sunshine every day to benefit from its vitamins. There is just something about sunshine that always lifts my spirits.

When you exercise, your body releases endorphins, which help to stabilize your mood. You will probably see improvements to your health, too. When we are stressed, our bodies release a hormone called cortisol. When we have too much of that hormone, we hold onto and store fat in our bodies. It can disrupt our sleep patterns, and it also causes other negative physiological effects on the body as well. Maintaining an active lifestyle can help fight that. Being active will not only help to stabilize your mood, but you will also be helping your body heal.

My third tip for you is to practice self-care. It's really important to make sure that you are incorporating self-care into your daily routine. This is one of the things that I let slip after my mom died. I think part of me felt like I didn't deserve to feel good. That simply isn't true, and your loved one would want you to take good care of yourself. I can still hear my mom asking me if I had eaten yet. She was lying in a hospital bed in pain, asking me if I had eaten anything. She always worried that I wasn't taking care of myself. She was right. It is important to take care of yourself. Adding in little things to treat yourself every day is super important. Take a mindful shower or bath. I like to add Epsom salts and essential oils to my bath. I also light a candle and turn on some good music or even an audiobook that I want to listen to. Speaking of books, another great idea is to relax with a good book or go have a spa day. Whatever it is that you enjoy doing the most, go do that. Schedule it in if you have to do that. Set an event in your phone to remind you to do something good for yourself.

It's important that you take extra care of yourself right now because you need it. Be gentle with yourself and have patience with yourself too. The grieving process is not easy. If it were easy, they would call it something like the grieving pie. You know, because we have the saying that something is as easy as pie. When you think about it, though, that honestly doesn't even make sense to me. Have you ever made a pie before? You have to make the dough, roll it out, and then make the filling. It's not easy! Anyway, you get my point. Grief is a difficult journey. Speaking of journeys, make sure you are getting enough sleep and eating in a healthy and balanced way. You're going to need it for that long journey. Please make sure you are eating. I feel like my mom is making me add that part. Many people stop doing that after they lose a loved one. I understand that when you are depressed, you may not feel like eating. Eat anyway. You don't want to get sick. You getting sick won't do anything to bring back your loved one. They wouldn't want you to be sick, either.

My fourth tip for you is to be of service to others. I know, I know…the last thing you want to do is volunteer your time. You don't have the energy or the motivation. I know… I get it…you're depressed. So, why am I recommending that you volunteer somewhere, other than the fact that I want to annoy you or give you a guilt trip? There are several reasons. I am so glad you asked. The first reason is that volunteering makes you feel good about yourself. When we help others, it gives us a sense of purpose and pride. Remember those endorphins that we talked about when you exercise. It's similar to that. You will also be taking the attention away from your own problems for a bit. It might give you a little perspective. You may see that other people are struggling even more than you are. You may realize that your life isn't so bad after all. It also feels fantastic when we can make someone else's life just a little better. You are making the world a better place. Just look at you. Another great reason to volunteer is that you could meet some really nice people in the process. You might make a lifelong friend. Isn't that what this world is really about? Helping others and making genuine human connections is why we're here. You'd be killing two birds with one stone.

Lastly, I want to state the importance of seeking professional help if you are feeling overwhelmed. Unfortunately, there is a stigma in this country when it comes to mental health. Most people believe that you should just get over your pain and sadness and move on with your life when tragedy happens. That isn't even close to a realistic or logical solution. Your body has a physical and emotional reaction to trauma. It actually changes the chemistry of your brain. Losing your loved one is a very traumatic event. Anyone who tells you that you should get over it, or that your grief shouldn't last this long, is an idiot. Grief doesn't have an expiration date. There is no set time for how long it will take or when you may feel better. You may feel better for a while and then feel bad again. Most companies will only give you 2 or 3 bereavement days, which I think is insane. If you need the extra time off, take it, and don't feel guilty for doing so. Don't let anyone tell you what an appropriate time to take off is. There is no formula for how to process your grief. What works for someone else may not work for you and vice versa. There is no instruction manual for how this is supposed to go. Have patience with yourself and this process. Seek help from others when you need it. We were not meant to go through this alone. We need to have a community to support us.

Your life may feel like it has a huge void in it right now. I know your life just isn't the same. After your loved one died, you probably had a wake and a funeral, or maybe your family sat Shiva. Your home was probably filled with loved ones and friends coming to support you and share their beautiful memories. Maybe they brought you food or flowers. Perhaps it comforted you for a bit. The problem is that the weeks following your loved ones death are usually pretty empty and lonely. The first few weeks are so busy, and you are still in shock. You have a constant flow of people checking on you.

It is after the initial shock wears off that the grief really sets in. People eventually stop checking on you and everyone tries to go back to life as usual, and they usually expect you to do the same. The only problem with that is the fact that your life will never be exactly the same again. I took a week off from school when my mom died. The district that I worked for gave us 3 bereavement days. I know that is standard practice, but 3 days to mourn the loss of a parent? That is insane. I needed 3 days just to plan the funeral. Unfortunately, our society does not properly support its grieving members. I took a week off, and I wasn't ready to go back even after a week. I felt so numb, and I didn't feel prepared to go back to life as usual. How was I expected to be positive in my classroom when all I wanted to do was cry? Even after my mom had been gone for several months, I would see reminders of her that would send me spiraling. Facebook would show me a memory, or I would see her name still listed as a profile on my Netflix account. There were constant reminders that she was no longer here, and it broke my heart just a little bit each time I saw something. I just wanted to curl up in a ball on the couch under a warm blanket. I wanted my mom to be there, hug me, and tell me everything would be ok. Except she wasn't there, and it didn't feel like it would ever be ok again.

Everyone expects you to just get over it. They don't say that, but they do expect you to go back to work and back to the normal routine. People say,

"You'll feel better if you get back to normal." The problem with that is now you have to figure out what your new normal even looks like. What is life as usual now, anyway? Maybe you had to make some serious adjustments in your life. After my mom passed, we had to sell our childhood home. That was a tough experience. Another tough experience was going to the doctor after she died and seeing her as my emergency contact. I immediately started sobbing, and then began thinking to myself…who will I call in an emergency now? Of course, I have people to call, but that is where my mind went after she died. I wondered who I would call if I needed help. I felt like an orphan even though I wasn't one. I still had my dad. I still had my siblings and my friends, yet my heart ached for that maternal guidance that I knew was now gone.

After my ex died, I wasn't sure how I was going to be able to afford the life that I knew. I was in full on panic mode about whether I could afford to keep my house. A lot of people don't understand that death can affect so many different aspects of your life. It can be very stressful and overwhelming. What I can tell you is that although things may never be normal again, what the heck is normal anyway, things will get easier with time. I'm not going to go into that time heals all wounds bullshit because we know that isn't really true. I'm simply saying that with time and a little perspective, things will get easier for you.

You may never be the same person you were before you lost your loved one. I know I am not. I will never be the same again. I don't think that is a bad thing. I think my mom's death has helped me to become a better person because now I value what truly matters. I am more empathetic to others who are struggling with loss. I also value life more than I did before. Before my mom's death, I found myself saying that I just wanted to skip through all of the days of the week until Friday. Can I just skip ahead until Friday? After her death, I realized how much of my life I was wishing away. It caused me to look at how I was showing up in the world. It made me do a review of my own life. Was I really happy? Was I doing everything I wanted to do? Now, I don't worry so much about a lot of things. When you lose a loved one, you start to see how much we worry over insignificant things. I put myself first now. If I need time off, I take it. If I need that weekend getaway, I go. Life is too short to be miserable.

Maybe this is a good time for you to do a life review. I always feel like we need to do these every few years anyway. Take a good look at your life and see what you need to add or take away from it. Less stress and more fun should be our everyday motto. Remember to take care of yourself like you would a dear friend. Depression won't last forever. Take each day one step at a time. Be gentle with yourself and be patient with your emotions as they come up. You are not crazy. This is just a really intense and painful journey. There will be peaks and valleys. Enjoy the good that comes to you in life, and know that the bad won't last forever. The sun always comes out again after the storm. You will see your loved one again. Until then, know that they are always with you. Love is eternal. It never dies. You are always one thought away from your loved one. Think of the happy memories and allow them to fill you with joy. Focus on all that you had instead of what you lost.

Remember that every little thing is going to be alright. Everything will be ok in the end, and if it's not ok, then it's not the end. You may be a little broken right now, but you will be whole again. Sometimes we have to be broken open in order to be put back together and made stronger than ever before.

CHAPTER 8

THE UPWARD TURN: MAYBE MY HEART WILL GO ON

O nce the depression starts to lift, you may begin to feel what grief professionals call "The Upward Turn." That's such a clever name, isn't it? It makes me think of a twist on a roller coaster. Hold on, we're about to go around the upward turn. Sorry, if you know me, you know that sarcasm is my love language. It's not my fault. I come by it naturally. My mom was the queen of sarcasm. In fact, she even had a look that we coined, "the LaVern look." We still joke that she is on the other side, giving people that look when they say something stupid. That actually comforts me so much to think that this is true. Anyway, now you may be starting to feel just a little bit better. That is definitely a step in the right direction. You are now entering "The Upward Turn" (cue dramatic music).

So, if it's not a roller coaster term, then what exactly is the upward turn? Here is how I define the Upward Turn stage. I noticed that I started to have the thought that maybe I could live another 30 years without my mom. Wow, now that I said that out loud, it sounds terrible. What I mean to say is that it occurred to me that there was just the slightest possibility that I might actually survive this horrible thing that happened. I didn't want to live without my mom, but I don't have a choice. She's not coming back anytime soon. Even though I don't want to live without her, I don't have to spend the next 30 years just waiting to die either. After all, if I am only focused on my mom's passing, then I am not really living. It was like a weight was lifted because once I finally accepted the fact that my mom wasn't coming back, I could begin to focus on my present and my future. I have so many blessings that are still around me. It was time that I started to notice them. It was time for me to think about what my next chapter could be. I could begin to move on with my life.

The phrase "move on with your life" instills a lot of guilt and fear in many people. I know that a part of me felt guilty in the beginning for thinking about all the things that I still had to look forward to without my mom. I felt like maybe we should freeze time and never experience anything fun since she couldn't be a part of it. In reality, my mom wouldn't want that for us. She would want us to continue living. I know that somewhere she is still a big part of our lives. I have so much to look forward to…my kids graduating from college, future grandkids, traveling, meeting the love of my life. The release of this book. There are so many amazing things still waiting for me. It has been my experience that many people experience guilt for moving on with their lives when their loved ones die. I know in my heart of hearts that our loved ones would want us to move on, and I know that they will be there for all the amazing things we experience in the future. My mom better show up! I think I just got the look. As a matter of fact, I know she will be there. She will just be there in a different form…in spirit.

After my mom first died, I couldn't focus on anything but my suffering and her death. I couldn't see the blessings surrounding me because of how much pain I was in. All I could focus on was the fact that I wouldn't have my mom in my life anymore and how unfair I thought it truly was. I was so hyper focused on what I had lost that I was ignoring what I still had. I remember thinking about everything my mom would miss. My niece Ginna even put together a TikTok video in memory of my mom that said, "Here are the things you missed this year." I see those kinds of tributes often on social media. It's great to remember your loved ones, but when you choose to focus solely on what will be missed, it only makes you incredibly sad and angry. I was angry that my mom wasn't going to see my kids graduate from college, and she wasn't going to see my niece and nephew graduate from high school. Keeping my attention on things like that didn't help me move through my grief. It only kept me in a constant state of negative emotion. I suddenly took on a victim mindset. Why did this happen to her? Why did this happen to me? This isn't fair. Life isn't fair. None of this is fair. Why did my mom have to die so young? I still needed her. It's incredibly easy to allow yourself to become immersed in that line of thinking, and your feelings are real and valid. Remember that our brains are hardwired to naturally gravitate toward the negative in life. It wasn't until I started shifting my perspective that things got easier for me. Don't misunderstand me. When I say easy, I don't mean that I don't get sad anymore or that I don't struggle sometimes. I simply mean that life doesn't feel so hopeless anymore. I am smiling more and choosing to prioritize happiness again.

I think an important thing to remember when you are going through this upward turn is not to feel guilty. It's OK to move on from your loved one's death. They would want you to do that. When I was a young girl, I loved the show The Facts of Life. Yes, I am dating myself. I am a proud child of the 80s. Our generation was so cool with our banana clips, Guess jeans, and Eastlands. I watched this show religiously and could probably quote most of the episodes. For those of you who are lame and have no idea what I am talking about…just kidding…the basic premise of the show is that 4 girls live together in a house with a woman who used to be their school's dietitian. Yes, the girls' parents were totally fine with their daughters living with a school dietitian. I know…it's a totally believable scenario, right?! Most TV shows from the 80s were. Remember the show Small Wonder? It was about a family whose dad brought home a robot from work that looked like a little girl. She was just a part of their family like any other sibling. No one ever questioned the family about this daughter with the robotic voice. What is a small wonder is how those writers survived all of the drugs they must have been doing to come up with those ideas.

I digress. There is a good reason that I am bringing up this show…even if I forgot what it was for a minute. What was it…oh yes, there is one episode that I will never forget. One of the characters was named Natalie. Her dad had died in a previous episode. In this particular episode, it was a few months after he died. The girls were throwing a party at the house. They were talking about the party, planning for it, and laughing. Natalie shied away from helping. She would make a joke. Her character was extremely sarcastic and always cracking jokes…that reminds me of someone. Everyone would laugh. She would then excuse herself and leave. During the party, she was alone in another room. Mrs. Garrett, the matriarch, came in and asked her why she was sitting alone. She said she felt guilty for having fun. Her dad was dead. She shouldn't be laughing. Mrs. Garrett then told Natalie a story. She explained that after her dad died, her friends took her to see a movie. She laughed for 2 hours, and then she went home and cried for 2 weeks. She wondered how she could be laughing when her father was dead. This was such a poignant moment because so often we think we have to be sad all the time when our loved ones die. We think that our loved ones will somehow be offended if we aren't grieving 24/7. We almost feel as though it's our duty to grieve all day every day.

The truth is that our loved ones do not want to see us in pain. Even if they were the type of person here on Earth who loved attention and drama or had narcissistic tendencies, they are not like that on the other side. Our loved ones want us to go on with our lives. They aren't sad on the other side because they can still visit us. I have connected to my mom many times since she has passed. I have spent time with her in dreams, she sends songs, and I have even felt her presence with me. You can connect to your loved ones too. Everyone has the ability. It's comforting to get signs from your loved one because it reminds you that we are only separated for a brief time. It just feels like an eternity to us here on Earth. We played a song at my mom's service that I absolutely love. It's called "Look For Me." The lyrics are so beautiful because they say, "When you finally make your entrance to that city of jasper walls and bright gold avenues. When you behold all its beauty and its splendor, remember there's just one request I'll make of you. Look for me, for I will be there too." This song is a reminder that this separation is only temporary. We will be together again with our loved ones, and what a grand reunion that will be. I know it can be tough to be patient and wait for that day, but the fact remains that we will be together again. It may be another 40 years before I see my mom. My brain can't even begin to fathom that right now, and if I try, it becomes incredibly sad. Instead, I choose to focus on the end result. In the end, we will all be together again. There will be no more sorrow and no more pain. There will be great rejoicing, which is something that I know I'm looking forward to.

Don't feel guilty for feeling good again. Don't feel bad for wanting to move on with your life. You're not really living if you are not moving forward. You aren't paying a great tribute to your loved one by staying stuck in life, either. They know you miss them, but there is still so much left for you to do here. Life goes on, and eventually you have to, as well. There are so many good things left in life. It feels good to laugh. It feels good to remember your loved one. They don't want us to remember how they were when they were sick, but one of the things that helped me shift my perspective when my mom died was remembering how much suffering she endured during her final days. My brother, sister, and I were at her bedside holding her hand as she took her final breath. I remember watching her as she labored so hard to take a breath. She wasn't conscious. I knew she was heavily sedated, so she wasn't in pain, but if she hadn't had that medication, she would have been so miserable. I watched her chest go up and down one final time, and I actually saw the light leave her eyes. I told my family that she was gone. "That was her last breath," I said when I knew that she had passed. I actually felt relieved because I knew that although her life had ended, her pain had ended too. Even when my ex-husband took his own life, I felt a sense of relief that he wasn't suffering from mental illness anymore either. In shifting the way we think about death, we are able to accept it and process it more easily.

The Upward Turn is actually a very good place to be. It's even better than an exciting roller coaster because it means that you are at a turning point in your grief. It means that you may be experiencing a sense of normalcy in your life. It means that you have hope that the future is still bright for you. You are absolutely correct. There are so many incredible experiences still ahead for you. My mom used to always dedicate a song to me called, "I Hope You Dance." In fact, we danced to it at my wedding. She always wanted me to experience life...to get out there...to dance. She wanted me to always be curious and adventurous. She hoped that I would take chances in life and live it fully. That is the true way that I can honor her memory. I can choose to keep dancing through life. I wish this for my daughter and son too, and they are so brave. My daughter chose to move 11 hours away to go to school because she loved the landscape. She was scared of being so far from home at first, but she took a chance anyway, and she loves it. My son has become a great leader where he works. I'm so proud of how he takes on new responsibilities. That is what life is all about. That is my hope for you too. I hope you always choose to look at life with wonder. I hope when amazing opportunities come your way, you take them. I hope you don't crawl under your blankets and hide from life. I hope you always choose to go out and dance.

CHAPTER 9

RECONSTRUCTION: CREATING YOUR NEW NORMAL, WHATEVER THAT IS

The next stage of grief is usually tied to the upward turn. That stage is called reconstruction and working through. When I first heard the name of this state, I pictured building a house. In a way, that is what you are doing. I love the shows on HGTV where they renovate old or ugly houses. It's so exciting to see what the finished product will be, and there are so many possibilities. The big reveal at the end is always extremely satisfying. In a way, you are just like that renovated house. Something ugly happened to you, and now you are building a new life for yourself. Just as those house renovation shows are on reality television, people like to think of this as the reality stage. Reality has set in. Your loved one is not coming back. The name of this stage is really perfect. You now have to make a new life for yourself because the life you knew no longer really exists. You may be starting to feel better. You have some glimmer of hope and are ready to move forward. You know that your life can and must go on, but now you have to decide what that will look like for you. I would like to clarify that when I say you feel better, I mean maybe you feel less like crap each day. I don't mean you feel like you won the lottery. Let's be honest, you may not feel completely normal again for a while. That is absolutely OK. Losing a loved one is tough, after all. I don't expect you to get through this quickly or easily, but there are some things to consider. We already discussed that you can't stop existing. You have to go on with your life and think about your future. So what exactly does your future hold? What will your new house or reality look like? That's what this stage is all about. It's time to figure that out.

Reconstruction is all about moving on with your life. When I say moving on, I don't mean leaving behind. Your loved one is always with you. They are still very much a part of your life. I would like to remind you that your loved one would want you to move on. Moving on doesn't mean forgetting them. It simply means that we are choosing to move forward and experience new things in our lives. I know people who completely stopped living after their loved one died. They wouldn't take any more family photos or go on vacations because their loved one couldn't be with them. Please don't stop living. You have other wonderful people left and so many amazing experiences yet to fulfill. You can't go back and change the past, and you can't freeze time. You can't crawl under a blanket and hide either…yes, you may want to. You can only get away with that for so long. People are going to start looking for you, and they will find you. I promise you that, and people can be so obnoxious. All humor aside, this is the part of our journey where we start to look at what our life will be like now that we have accepted our loved one's death and are moving forward. What will our new normal be? Moving forward in life may look very different for each person. If you lost a spouse, this could include dating again (If this is you, I am so sorry because dating in today's world really sucks…see my previous book and the chapter on dating again), or maybe you downsize your home and move into a smaller space. Maybe you never lived on your own, and now you have to figure out how to pay your bills or run your household. If you lost a child, maybe you finally decide to go and clean out your child's room, or maybe you donate their old clothes. Maybe this is the first time you've even been able to go into their room…baby steps. What matters most is that you start to think about how you will move forward with your life.

After losing my mom, I had to make some major adjustments. I no longer had the same daily routine, and my family dynamic changed drastically. Before my mom's death, I would text her during the day and then go to her house in the evening to help take care of her. I had a lot of time open up after she passed, and I didn't really know what to do with myself at first. Another major life transition for me was that my children went off to college, so l found myself experiencing a lot of loneliness when my mom first died. I went from a life full of family to being by myself a lot. I found myself falling into a depression. That depression could have gotten much deeper, but I decided to do something about it. I was going to use the free time I now had to my advantage. I wanted to shift my focus in my career. I had been dreaming about working on more creative projects. I decided that this was the perfect time to do just that. This book is one of those projects. I realized that I wanted to use my painful experience to help people. I also wanted to travel more, and I got my wish. I took my first cruise, visited places I had never been before, and I crossed a few things off of my bucket list. That is the point of this stage. It's a time of discovery and curiosity and a time of growth and expansion. It's about deciding that you are going to make the most out of life and figuring out what that looks like for you. If we learn any lesson at all from death, may it be that life is precious and short. Experience all that you can, and live your life to the fullest. I don't think that anyone ever says on their deathbed that they were glad they stayed home and never traveled. Get out there and experience life.

Depending on who you lost, this phase might be quite difficult. It may create huge change for you, or it may not bring a lot of change for you. Whatever that looks like for you is going to be unique to you. This stage may simply mean that you decide to get up and participate in the world again. Maybe you plan that next trip or enroll in that college course. As I mentioned earlier, my daughter decided to change schools. She transferred to a school in Colorado. She had always wanted to go but put it on hold when her dad died. She needed to experience a new setting. She wanted to explore her dream of going to school in a beautiful mountain setting. Although I was worried at first, I knew I had to put my worry aside and let her go.

I knew it would be difficult having her so far away, but you are never really that far away when technology can connect you. My son decided to put a great deal of his energy into work. He struggled with motivation after his dad died, and it is not difficult to understand why. I'm proud of him for deciding to fight his depression and make his own way in life. It was a huge step for him. Whatever you choose to do, remember this one thing–have patience and be gentle with yourself during this process.

Sometimes this stage requires us to truly look at our lives and figure out who we are and what we want out of life. Most of us are so busy that we go through life on autopilot. We end up in jobs, relationships, or situations that do not feel truly fulfilling. It can be stifling, and we can often feel stuck in a rut. We get to a point in life where we really don't know what we want out of life or what will make us happy. Having to figure that out isn't always easy. Perhaps you can take this opportunity to explore your interests and try new things. You never know what can happen when you do. I decided to take a free course on HTML coding. I have always wanted to try it and thought it might be something enjoyable. I was right. I learned a lot and more importantly, it made me feel highly accomplished to try something new. Enjoying it was just a bonus. Am I going to make a career out of coding? No. That wasn't the point of taking the class. The reason I took it was to try something new that piqued my interest. What is something that you have always wanted to try? If time and money were no object, what would you do? Maybe spend a little time coming up with some ideas. Create a list of ideas, and then pick one or two of them to try. It can be fun and exciting to open yourself up to new adventures.

I challenge you to examine what you want your life to look like. Are you already living your ideal life? If not, why not? What do you need to do more or less of in order to make that happen? Life is too short to feel stressed. Life should be joyful. What would make your life more enjoyable? Maybe you want to travel more. Perhaps you feel called to change careers. It doesn't have to be such a major life change. It could be something as simple as trying a new hobby. Maybe, like my daughter, you need a change of scenery. Whatever it is, this is the perfect time to explore everything. You already have to reconstruct your life. Why not make your remaining years the best years yet? Imagine for a minute that they renovated a house on one of those HGTV shows, but all they did was change out a light fixture and paint. We would all be so underwhelmed, and I'm sure the ratings for that show would drop. That's the point. Don't live a life that is underwhelming. Figure out what would make your life amazing, what would make others think, "Wow, what a glow up!" Some people fear change, and that is a very human experience. Change can be scary. The unknown can be intimidating, but it doesn't have to be. Mindset absolutely matters.

You can focus on all the things that could go wrong, or you can focus on the benefits of the new experience. Don't allow fear to keep you paralyzed or stuck in life. Sometimes you have to just do things scared. There is a famous quote that says, "The definition of insanity is doing the same thing over and over again and expecting different results." If you want to experience life, you have to branch out and try new things. If fear is keeping you from doing that, then you need to tackle that fear. I talked about tapping before, but it is a great way to release some of the fear we experience. It's also important to look at each fear individually. Is your fear rational or not? Most of the time our fears are irrational. We talk ourselves out of doing a lot of things in life merely because we let our fear convince us that we won't be successful. When we do that, we let fear win.

I have already talked about how much I love journaling because I think it allows us to really examine our thoughts, feelings, and our behaviors. During this stage, I think it's a great idea to really reflect on your life. Are there things you need to change? Oftentimes, a death can make us realize just how precious and valuable life really is. If your life isn't where you want it to be, it's time to look at why or what you can do to change that. Sometimes even the littlest adjustment to our lives can make a huge difference.

I'd like to offer an exercise for you. First, find some quiet, uninterrupted time to sit with a journal. Next, ask yourself the following questions:

- What is the hardest part of my day?

- Is there anything I can do to make that part of my day easier?

- What is the best part of my day?

- What can I do more of in order to create more happiness in my day?

- What is worrying me right now?

- What would I love to do more of right now?

- Is there anything holding me back from trying something new today?

- What thoughts or behaviors do I need to let go of right now?

- What can I add to my life to make it more enjoyable?

- Do I need help from my support system right now? Am I comfortable asking for it?

The answers to these questions will help you to understand what you can do to move forward in life. Another tool that I love using is a vision board. These are so fun because you can be creative with them. What do you want to see in your own life? Do you want a new car, a new job, a new house, a new partner? What do you want? The possibilities are endless and are only limited by your imagination. You can either create a physical vision board, or you can create a virtual one.

If you are creating a physical vision board, then you will need to get a poster board and some photos. Cut out pictures of the items you want to add to your vision board and paste them onto your board. I prefer creating a virtual vision board using Pinterest. I create a separate board for each area of my life. I have one for my dream home, one for career, and one for travel. I then add photos or quotes to that board. The photos are of what I want my life to look like in that particular area. The quotes are how I want to feel in my life, and they keep me motivated. I look at my boards every few days and try to imagine what it would feel like to have all of those things in my life. Have fun creating your boards and imagine how amazing your life would be if you had those things. It's really fun to daydream. Daydreaming is also a very intense manifesting tool because our thoughts are so powerful. Also, having a vision board helps you to stay focused on your goals.

Like a Phoenix rising from the ashes, you can create a beautiful new life out of the remains of the old one. Your life can still be amazing. The first part of my life was not easy. I had to learn lesson after lesson. It was pretty exhausting. I know that because I have done a lot of healing work in the first half of my life, the second half is going to be filled with the rewards from my hard work. Your second half, or quarter, or however long you have, can also be amazing. In fact, I know it will be, and your loved one will be right there cheering you on.

Here is a prayer for new beginnings:

Dear Archangel Michael,

I humbly ask you to direct my path. Help me to face my fears head on, trusting that the Universe is working on my behalf. Lead me to new opportunities and give me the courage to walk through new doors. Please bring people onto my path who can help me to move forward in life. Protect me and help me to feel safe as I embark on this new path.

Amen

CHAPTER 10
ACCEPTANCE: FACING THE COLD
HARD TRUTH

Once you have dealt with your new normal and the reality of restructuring your life, you come to the final stage of grief, which is acceptance. When I hear the word acceptance, I think…fine. I didn't want this, but it happened, so I guess I'll deal with it. It reminds me of the story my aunt used to tell me about the day my sister and I were born. This was before they did ultrasounds for pregnant women. There was no grandiose gender reveal party. You barely knew if you had an actual baby in there. Ah, the good ole days. The day we were born was extremely chaotic. The doctor told the nurse to mark this one baby A. My dad knocked over a chair. Everyone was overjoyed that my mom had delivered twins. We were the first twins born at our new local hospital, so it was all the more exciting. When they told my brother that my mom had twin girls, he said, "All I wanted was one brother, and instead I got two sisters." Life is unfair, kid. Needless to say, he was not as overjoyed as everyone else.

Just like my brother, you were dealt this horrible hand, and now you know you're stuck with it. My brother was stuck with us too, but he learned to love and appreciate his two sisters, at least I think he did. My point is that you can learn to love and appreciate where you are, too. Well, maybe you don't have to love it, but you can at least appreciate that this is not the end of your world. There are still so many amazing things left to experience in life. My son and I were talking recently, and I said to him, "I know it isn't fair that you've had to deal with so much trauma at such a young age. You can either play the victim and stay wounded your whole life, or you can decide that you're going to heal from it." He said that he was tired of feeling bad. He wanted to heal. I think that is an incredibly brave thing to do. Healing is never easy, but it is necessary if you want to be truly happy in life. In my opinion, acceptance is the catalyst that truly sparks healing, and it is an extremely important part of the journey.

Acceptance does not always equal happiness. It doesn't mean that you immediately feel better. It was more gradual than that for me. My brother didn't love us immediately either. It took him some time to warm up to us…only about 20 years or so. You've been through a lot of pain and turmoil. You may not return to the carefree you that you were for a while, but you will get through this. You will find your way forward. A time will come that when you think about your loved one, you will smile instead of cry. Eventually, it doesn't rip your heart out to think about them. I again go back to the saying that time heals all wounds. I would change that statement to say, "Time allows us to gain a new perspective." The more that time passes, the easier it is to see things differently.

Now, instead of asking, "Why did my mom have to die?", I say, "I'm glad I had the time I had with her." I'm learning to appreciate what I had instead of focusing on what I lost. Even though your life may never be the same again, there is fresh hope that there are so many more beautiful things left to experience in this life.

What does one experience during the acceptance stage? A few of the characteristics of the acceptance stage are as follows. You may feel an increase in positivity and hopefulness. Now that you understand that there is more life out there for you, you may feel hopeful. Perhaps before this stage, you didn't know how you could go on or even see a future without your loved one. You now realize that you have to move forward, even if you aren't sure how to at first. You may begin to seek out new meaning in life and search for the answers to life's questions. The death of a loved one often sparks a spiritual awakening in many people. You may begin to question your religion or spirituality. Death often leaves people wondering what happens to us after we die. These are all valid and important questions, and it can be very healing to research the answers to these questions.

You may also begin to feel more secure in life. After you realize that you can survive this, you begin to feel more relaxed and at ease. Maybe in the beginning, you didn't know how you would be able to move on without your loved one. I know when my ex-husband died, I wasn't sure if I would be able to make it financially. I slowly began to realize that I would be fine. Once you finally accept that, you will survive. You will be OK. You begin to engage with reality as it is and not how you thought it would be. I never thought that I would be without my mom for the rest of my life. Now, I think about who my support system currently is. I no longer think, "How will I deal with this without my mom?" Instead, I think, "I will call this person if this happens." I have had to face the reality of who I have left in my circle. Even though my circle has gotten smaller, I still have a support system that is there when I need it.

You may start to become more mindful and present in your everyday life. This is so important. We miss out on so much when we live life on autopilot. I felt like I was mentally checked out in life for so long after my mom died. It was the only way I could get through the day for a while. I knew I had to stop going through the motions and start living again. You will begin to cope and adapt to your current circumstances. Once you do that, you are more able to tolerate your emotions and begin to be more open and vulnerable. You can start communicating in an honest and open manner. For some people, it is hard to be vulnerable after a loss. Talking about it really does help. It's also critical to start taking care of yourself again. It is good to do nice things for yourself. You deserve to feel good again. You can also begin to stop feeling guilty about being happy because you know that your loved one would want you to have a wonderful life.

You may be experiencing all of these things or some of these things, and perhaps you are just beginning to experience this stage. Wherever you are is perfectly acceptable. I like to tell my coaching clients, "You may not be where you want to be yet, but you are not where you were yesterday." In other words, you have already come so far in this healing journey. You may not be completely healed yet, so have patience with yourself and this process. To be perfectly honest, healing is a lifelong process. You may not feel completely better yet, but you have already done so much of the work.

You are already on the road to recovery. You need to appreciate and congratulate yourself for the progress that you have made. This journey is hard. It's not for the faint of heart. Not everyone survives it if we're being completely honest. Some people never move on with their lives. They stay stuck in sadness and pain because they can't seem to find their way forward, or in the worst case scenario, I have seen people take their own life because they can't bear to go on without their loved one. If you are reading this book, I know you want to feel better. Look at what an amazing job you are doing. The world still needs you. Keep shining your beautiful light. If, however, you are contemplating suicide, please reach out for help. There is no shame at all in admitting that you are struggling. You are not alone. There are so many wonderful organizations who are around to help you. You can call the suicide prevention hotline at 988, or you can visit their website at https://988lifeline.org/ for more resources. Remember that no one fights alone.

Healing is not always an easy process, but you are doing a great job. Here are some tips to help you keep this amazing momentum going. First, remember that this process takes time. Rome was not built in a day, and your healing will not happen that fast either. Continue to have patience with yourself and this journey. If you do have a bad day, and we all do from time to time, don't feel guilty or ashamed. One bad chapter isn't the end of the book. You can turn the page, and tomorrow there will be a new chapter. My friend and I were sitting down to dinner a few nights ago. My mom has been gone for over a year. She mentioned a song that someone said reminded them of my mom. We both started crying right there in that restaurant. You will still have triggers, and that is OK. Don't feel bad because it's been over a year or two years or ten years, and you are still sad. That is the way it works. I don't think the pain and sadness ever truly go away because the love never goes away. Sadness is just your love spilling out all over the place. With time, those emotions become more manageable.

One tool that really helps in redirecting our thoughts is affirmations. I love affirmations because they help us to shift our mindset, which in turn shifts our reality. Try using some of these affirmations when those negative thoughts creep up on you. I am at peace with myself. I accept everything in my life. I accept the little gifts that are strewn throughout my life. I accept the power of the Universe. I know that there are amazing blessings just ahead. I see the good in my life. I trust that there is more good yet to come.

Remember to surround yourself with the people and things that you love. Draw them in closer instead of isolating yourself from them. We need people. It's who we are. We are emotional beings who rely on community with others. So, start embracing your tribe. It's also important to shift your perspective a little. Focus on the positive things that are happening in your life. There is always a reason to be grateful. Focus on what you still have rather than what you lost. As a teacher, the school year can sometimes become unbearable. Right around February or March, I start to think, "I can't do this anymore. I need to find a new career." "There are too many days left in the school year." "I'm not going to make it." For those of you who are not educators, this is around the time of year that students stop working.

Their behavior becomes terrible, and they are ready to be done with school. The problem is that we still have four months left. What I have discovered is that if I focus on the next positive thing, it is manageable and bearable. For example, I will focus on getting through until the next day off. I only have to make it until Friday. Next week we have spring break. I just need to get through a few more days. If I focused on having four months left, I would have a mental breakdown. I have to focus on the positives in life and take things one day at a time, one step at a time, one moment at a time. That is what you must do now too.

Remember the courage and resilience that you have shown in these times of trial. You have done such an amazing job. If you are here reading this book, it probably means that you are seeking help. You want to feel better, and you want to heal. That is a huge step in the right direction. I know a lot of people who never heal from wounds they don't speak about. In fact, I think you are so brave for facing your wounds. The raw reality is that you have to be ready to heal, and sometimes it takes a hot minute. You can't force anyone else to heal if they aren't ready. So, the mere fact that you are on your healing journey is amazing. You should celebrate all the progress you make. Healing is one of the most difficult challenges we face in life, and I believe it is one of the biggest reasons we come here. We come here to learn how to heal from the things that almost break us. Most people don't even realize that they need to heal, so the fact that you are doing it is incredible.

If I could leave you with one thing about acceptance, it is this. Acceptance does not mean that we forget our loved ones. It doesn't mean that we hide their pictures in a box and never think about them again, or that we hide all the other evidence that they ever existed. Acceptance means that we understand that our loved one is no longer here with us and has taken on another form. The love we shared never dies.

As long as you hold that love in your heart, your loved one never truly dies, either. It is not easy to move forward with your life, but it is necessary. We can't curl up in a ball on the couch, remaining frozen in time. I mean, technically, you could do that. Would you really want to? Yes, you will have days when all you want to do is curl up on the couch crying your eyes out, or you may spend the day doing nothing but zoning out and watching trash TV. That's ok, too. Life is about finding balance. So, some days you will be a hot mess, and other days you will be amazing. The takeaway here is that we have to go on. We simply don't have a choice. Life does not stop for our grief. We still have to continue to pay our bills, care for our loved ones, and take care of ourselves. That doesn't stop just because we are sad. If you ever find yourself feeling guilty about moving on, think about this. What would you want your loved one to do if something happened to you? Would you want them to remain stuck and miserable in life? I would hope not. You would want your loved one to have a beautiful life. You will have moments that may seem unbearable. Don't forget that it is important to pay attention to your emotions and honor them. It's perfectly OK to take a break when you need it. You're human, not a cold robot. You will need a timeout on occasion. There are days when I come home from school that I just sit on the couch for 15-20 minutes doing nothing. I have to completely reset from my day. My energy is completely drained. Grief is extremely draining energetically. You may have days like that, too. Finding your way through grief can be taxing. Remember to give yourself grace.

One truly important reminder that we all need is to be our own advocate. If you need a mental health break, by all means take it. Be kind, gentle, and patient with yourself. If you need help, ask for it. People are not mind readers, and they sometimes forget that grief takes a long time. They get busy and forget to ask us how we are doing or if we need anything once the funeral has passed. It's your job to know when you need help and to ask for it. Things will get easier. With each passing day, the pain will begin to ease. There is always purpose in our pain. It's teaching us some very valuable life lessons, whether we want to admit it or not. Death teaches us to value what is important in life and to let go of what is not. Keep that lesson, but try to lose the pain attached to it. Life is messy, but it is also extremely beautiful.

Keep those sweet memories close, and go out and make some new ones. You have so many amazing adventures waiting for you, but you have to keep living in order to experience them. Your loved one can still be very much a part of the rest of your life. I choose to talk about my mom so that I can keep her always close. It's a way for me to remember her every day. When something reminds me of her, I share it. I miss her terribly, but as long as I have those amazing memories, she is still with me. In the next chapter, I'm going to talk about how we can feel our loved ones around us and ask for signs from them. Remember this...love is all that is real. Love never dies.

Love is all we take with us when we leave this world, and your loved ones want you to know that you are deeply loved.

Here is a prayer for acceptance:

Dear Universe,

Help me to accept what I cannot change. Give me the courage and the wisdom to make adjustments in my life for the better. Allow me to trust in my own intuition as it guides me to beautiful things. May I be in flow of life. May I see the beauty that surrounds me everyday.

Amen

CHAPTER 11

ASKING FOR SIGNS: CONNECTING TO THE LOVE THAT STILL EXISTS

When our loved ones pass away, the love that they have for us doesn't die with them. It still very much exists. In fact, that is the only thing they take with them when they leave. They no longer need their worn out bodies because they are now just a soul. They are a big ball of beautiful energy. They are pure love and light. We are living in the physical 3D dimension, while our loved ones are now in the 5D. They are no longer weighed down by all of the things that weigh us down here on Earth. Their soul lives on in this new dimension. It simply resides on another energetic plane…one that is a higher energetic frequency than ours. Some people call this plane heaven; whatever you call it, it is a beautiful space where only love truly exists. Although your loved one is no longer present in the 3D space, we can still communicate with them. We can ask our loved ones to send us signs to show us that they are still with us. They love letting us know that they are around, and there are many ways that they do this.

One of the ways that my mom comes through to us is through music. Music was her life. She started singing from a very young age.She directed the youth choir in her church. As she got older, she preferred to sing country music. She was especially fond of Patsy Cline. She would sing her songs when she performed at local festivals, singing contests, and at karaoke. Everyone loved her singing, and she used to joke that she sang Patsy's songs more than Patsy herself did. One evening she made her presence known in a very definitive way just a week after she died. My daughter was driving home from visiting my house. She was 20 at the time, and her music preference was current music like Panic at the Disco. She definitely did not listen to country...ever. She had her Spotify app on when "Crazy" by Patsy Cline started playing. She called me immediately and said, "That had to be Nana." I truly believe it was. The chances of that particular song playing on Ally's Spotify list were pretty slim. Another fascinating thing was that the song "Crazy" became a popular background song for TikTok videos just weeks after my mom died. That song was popular in 1961... over sixty years ago. Although many people know this song, it's relatively unknown to people who do not listen to country music. Coincidence? I think not.

Another way that our loved ones can connect with us is through nature. After my mom died, we had hummingbirds. I had never seen a hummingbird in my yard before, and I have lived in my house for over 11 years. It flew right up to my face and hovered there. I know this was my mom. In another instance, my yard was full of dragonflies. I've seen one or two dragonflies in my yard before. This was a pack of dragonflies.

I've never seen that many together in my entire life, let alone in my yard. Many people see cardinals or butterflies and know that their loved ones are near. Speaking of butterflies, I just recently had an incredible experience with a butterfly. My niece and I were at the zoo. An interesting thing to note is that my mom loved going to the zoo with us, especially after she got sick. She loved sitting in the sunshine on a warm day. My sister's family and I went to the butterfly garden in the zoo. A big yellow butterfly landed right on my niece's arm. My mom loved the color yellow. I don't know if I have ever seen a yellow butterfly in person before. I just had to snap a photo. My niece was a little afraid of the butterfly being on her arm, so I stuck my finger out to it. It jumped right onto my finger, and we got a few more really cool photos. She was absolutely trying to tell us that she was with us. I have so many wonderful pictures of my mom with us at the zoo. I believe it was her way of letting us know that she still goes there with us.

Many people have had strange occurrences with their pets. The reason for this is that animals are extremely sensitive to Spirit. There are times when my dogs will stare in the corner, and they act like someone is there. Spirits love to use animals to try to get our attention. Children see spirits as well, as they are also very sensitive to energy. Pay attention if your children start talking about seeing departed loved ones because it is most likely that they are seeing them. Another thing that spirits like to do is mess with electricity. I will never forget something that happened the day after my mom's funeral. The whole family got together at our friend Lori's house. We were all talking when the lights above us and the TV went out for a minute and then came back on. We laughed and said, "OK, LaVern, we know you're here." That's the thing about my mom. She loved a good party. She definitely would have been there at the center of the conversation. She was so funny and charismatic and could hold anyone's attention.

You may find that your electronic devices go a little haywire when a loved one passes. This is because spirits can manipulate electricity. After my great aunt Gee died, a friend of mine posted a song on Facebook for me to let me know she was thinking of me in my time of grief. It was a YouTube video. My phone was laying on my bed in the locked screen position. I would have had to unlock it using the face ID or by entering a code. I also would have needed to open the Facebook and YouTube app in order for the video to play. I left the room to go grab something, and I heard music playing. When I walked back into my room, that video was playing on my phone. I still don't know how it could have been playing. This was at a time when YouTube would not continue playing a video if you closed the app. Not only was my phone locked, but the YouTube app was closed as well. I'm so impressed by how she made that happen. I knew that my aunt was letting me know she was around me. This is the same aunt who prayed for me every night, so it makes sense that she would show up to say hi.

Other ways that our loved ones can show up for us is through items they leave in our path. They can put feathers, coins, or other objects around us to let us know that they are near. Ask your loved one to leave you a specific sign, and then watch as amazing things start to happen. I have been finding quarters since my mom died. I find that hilarious because most relatives leave pennies. Not my mom. Pennies aren't good enough for her kids. Some people say that they find heart shaped objects around when they think of their loved ones. Whatever object you find, you will know when it's from your loved one.

Our loved ones can even visit us in our dream state. If you dream of them, and it feels very real, it was probably a visitation from them. When our brains are in an alpha state, it is easier for us to connect with our loved ones. The reason that it is so difficult for us to see and hear our loved ones when we are awake is because of the difference in our energetic frequencies. It would be like trying to get a satellite television signal through thick brick with lots of trees around. You may get a fuzzy picture, but you can't get the best reception. We have to raise our vibration, and they have to lower theirs in order for us to meet in the middle.

Perhaps you have visited a medium trying to connect with your loved one, or maybe you would like to do that. I had a few sessions with a medium after my mom passed. I was so distraught from watching her suffer, and I knew she was afraid to die. I needed to hear for myself that she was OK. It was especially comforting to hear messages of love from her, but you really don't have to visit a medium to get your own messages. You can do this without a medium because we all have the ability to connect to our loved ones on the other side. You may not believe me, but it's true. We were all born with the ability to connect to the other side. I think mediums are very talented and can provide much needed comfort and validation after a loved one passes, but you could go into debt easily if the only way you could connect was through a medium. I know you want to feel connected to your loved one as much as possible. The good news is that you can.

You can absolutely go to a medium to connect with your loved one. If you do decide to visit a medium, it's important to understand how to find mediums that are honest. We have a local fair where the mediums have to be vetted before they can participate. Do a Google search for local psychic fairs. That's a good place to start because legitimate business people do not want a reputation for scamming people. They tend to make sure that the vendors at their fairs are on the up and up.

If you want to try tapping into your own gifts, then I would like to give you some helpful tips for how to connect with your loved one yourself. Connecting with our loved ones is something that can be very healing.

We can get physical proof that our loved ones are still very much a part of our lives and with us. It can also help to hear that our loved ones are not suffering and that they still love us. Some of the activities that I am going to teach you will require you to open up your mind and tap into your intuitive abilities. It's a popular belief that only special people are born with psychic gifts. That simply isn't true. We all have them. Most of us have just ignored them or didn't realize what those gifts actually are.

If you need proof that we can connect to the other side, just look to children. There have been many books written about children and some of the things they have to say about heaven or spirits. Wayne Dyer wrote a book called *Memories of Heaven* in which children recall heaven before they ever came here. They recall picking their parents, and some even recall past lives where they were once the parent and their now parent was their child. There is even a television show called *The Ghost Inside My Child,* which contains stories of children who remember being someone else in a past life.

These stories are often backed up by facts that can be researched. One child even remembered designing the Titanic. He drew pictures of it with a fourth smokestack, which most people are unaware that the Titanic had because it was a dummy smokestack.

In the book *Memories of Heaven*, there are also stories of children who are visited by deceased relatives. I experienced one such incident when my daughter was 2. It was our normal nighttime routine for me to rock her and sing to her before bed. One night, as I was rocking her, she started giggling and waving at something in the corner. It was just the two of us sitting in the living room. She then pointed and said, "Papa Til." She called my dad's partner Papa Til because she couldn't say Phil, so I just thought she was remembering him. I forgot about it until the next time we went to my grandma Lassen's house. There was a photo of my grandpa sitting on top of my grandma's entertainment center. Ally pointed to the picture and said, "Papa Til." My grandpa died before I was born. I never knew him in this lifetime. My daughter knew exactly who my grandpa was. There was no doubt about it. He was there with us the night that I was rocking her, and she saw him clearly. She saw him vividly enough that he was making her laugh. I later had a medium tell me that there was a grandpa always around me and my daughter. I already knew that. As children, we can connect easily to our loved ones on the other side. It's when we get older that we are told it isn't possible and/or our abilities seem to weaken or disappear. We get told that we are simply hearing or seeing things. You may have heard someone tell you that it was just your imagination. I was told I had an imaginary friend when I was little. I'm pretty sure now that it was a spirit guide.

Anyone can connect to the other side. You simply have to be willing and open to using the gifts you already have. Even if you think you don't have any gifts, I would be willing to bet that you have experienced things you can't explain that would prove otherwise. You are most likely connecting to Spirit without realizing it. In the next few paragraphs, I'm going to give you some activities that you can do starting right now to help you connect more to your intuition, which will in turn help you connect to Spirit. Before you start practicing, though, it's important to let go of fear. Most people block their intuitive gifts because they are afraid of them. Throughout history, there have been individuals who had spiritual gifts who were considered to be witches or other negative beings. They were often persecuted for it. This led to many people ignoring or shutting off their spiritual gifts. This is another reason that you need to let go of the fear surrounding the other side. Maybe this is something completely new to you. That is perfectly fine. Just go slow. Take this one step at a time.

You have nothing to be afraid of. You are going to learn how to set the intention that you are only connecting to loving beings. There is nothing to fear because we are not inviting any negative spirits in. You are simply connecting to receive a comforting message from those you love. Tell yourself that it is safe for you to hear, it is safe for you to see, and it is safe for you to know what your loved ones want to communicate to you. You may only get a small message when you start, or you may get nothing at first.

That doesn't mean it isn't working. It takes practice to break down the years of barriers that we have put up around our gifts.

The first step in connecting to your gifts is to connect to your intuition. We all have an internal GPS called our intuition, and we can all connect to our intuition in different ways. Most of the time, we do not even realize that we are using our intuition. So, how do you know what your intuition is or if you are using it? In order to understand the answer to that, I need to explain what intuition is. According to the Oxford Dictionary, intuition is defined as "the ability to understand something immediately, without the need for conscious reasoning." We are able to understand things in a variety of ways. In fact, there are four main types of intuition. We are usually stronger in one or two types over the others, but you can strengthen your ability to connect to each type of intuition.

The first type of intuition is clairaudience, or clear hearing, which refers to hearing voices or sounds. I have, on occasion, experienced clairaudience. There were a few interesting interactions that happened to me when I was trying to go to sleep at night. In one instance, I was laying in bed trying to go to sleep when I distinctly heard my mom say my name. It sounded like she was right next to me. I wasn't asleep, but I heard it so clearly. She had already passed away at this point. I think she was trying to get my attention. A similar thing happened to me with my great Aunt.

I heard her say my name so clearly. She was still living at this point, so I was a little confused about why I heard her say my name. The next time I saw her, she said, I pray for you every night. I know I was hearing her say my name when she prayed. It was like we had a connection that went beyond this physical world. I also heard my ex-husband say my name one night. He was still alive then, too. I called him immediately and asked him if he was talking about me. He laughed and asked why I asked that question. He said that he did say my name. It's so interesting how you can be so connected to people who are not physically with you. The way that you know you are connecting to your loved one through clairaudience, and you are not crazy is that you will hear messages in their voice, not yours. Also, the messages will never be scary or harsh. It's usually a gentle, loving message, or in my case, my name.

How do you know if this is the intuition that you might connect to the most? There are a few signs. Do you hear sounds when others are around that they don't hear? This could be hearing your name called or hearing an animal. Maybe you hear music. Do you talk to yourself frequently? Oftentimes, we talk to ourselves to process what we are thinking. Perhaps you get guidance by talking to yourself. Do you find when you do this that answers come to you without you really understanding where they are coming from? Did you talk to an imaginary friend as a child? Do you crave peace and quiet? Do you regularly hear ringing, high-pitched or unusual noises? If you answered yes to any of these questions, then clairaudience might just be the way that you are connecting to your intuition.

What can you do to strengthen this ability? Clairaudience is associated with the 5th energy chakra. We have 7 main energy chakras in the body. *Chakra* in Sanskrit means *wheel*. Each chakra is a wheel of energy, and each chakra is associated with something different. The 5th chakra is the throat chakra. It is located in the center of your throat. This chakra deals with speaking your truth. Singing or what is called toning is a great way to strengthen this chakra. Meditation is another great way to strengthen this chakra. There are guided meditations for clearing the throat chakra that are very helpful. Just do a YouTube search for a throat chakra clearing guided meditation. Another activity that you can do to strengthen your clairaudience abilities is to practice sitting in stillness. To do this, find a quiet space, close your eyes, take a deep breath, and ask the Universe, your guides, or even your departed loved one to send you a message. Now set a timer for three minutes and just listen. Notice any sounds that come in for you. If you don't get anything the first time you try it, that is OK. As with anything, the more you practice, the better you become. You may need to do this several times before you are able to hear anything.

The next type of intuition is claircognizance, or clear knowing. This is the type of intuition that is the strongest for me. I get thoughts that pop into my head, but I know they are not coming from my brain. I just know things. For example, a client will ask me a question about their job. The answer pops into my head. I don't have any way of knowing about my client's job. I don't research anyone before I meet with them. I don't have time to do that. I will get thoughts that pop into my head like… I know you are unhappy at your job. There is a boss who makes you feel like you aren't good enough. You wish you could find something else. The client is amazed that I knew that.

That isn't exactly something you can look up on Facebook. I don't know how I know. I just do. Sometimes I will receive guidance that is so strong. I don't know where exactly it is coming from. I just know that I need to follow it. After my mom died, I asked to receive messages from her. I got thoughts that popped into my head like, "I love you, and I am proud of you." I know she wanted me to know those things. I trusted that it was from her. Your ego may try to tell you that what you are experiencing isn't real, but I can assure you that it is. The more you practice this skill, the better you are able to connect to it.

How do you know if you connect more to your intuition with claircognizance? You tend to just know things. Ideas just pop into your head. You receive guidance that you know you have to follow. How can you develop this type of intuition more? One practice is to take a few moments to sit in stillness and practice free writing. You will need a pen and paper for this exercise. Find a quiet place and plan on devoting 15-20 minutes to this exercise. Once you get comfortable in a quiet setting, you can begin. First, close your eyes, take a deep breath, and ask to receive information. It can be a specific question that you ask, like what is the name of my spirit guide, or you can simply ask to get a message. Then write whatever comes to your mind. It took me a while to realize that what I was getting was not coming from me. The only way I was finally able to trust it was that I practiced with other people. I asked to get information about someone else. Then I wrote down whatever I was receiving. I told the person what I got, and it was always correct. It was also information that I could not have known about that person beforehand, like how they were feeling that day.

Strengthening your crown chakra or the 7th chakra, which is associated with our connection to the Divine, Divine love, and inner knowing and is located at the top of our head, can help to strengthen this form of intuition. There are guided meditations on YouTube for clearing the crown chakra. Another way to clear this chakra is to hold crystals. You can carry them with you, or put them on your crown chakra when you meditate. The crystals most associated with the crown chakra are amethyst, moonstone, and clear quartz. I also really like using blue kyanite when I try to connect to the crown chakra.

The next form of intuition is clairvoyance or clear sight. As the name suggests, when you connect using this form of intuition, you can see things. Sometimes people with this ability can actually see spirit, or at least they may see light and colors. Others can see images that pop into their head. It may even appear as though you are seeing a movie in your head. One way to strengthen this type of intuition is to sit quietly with your eyes open. Focus on an object that doesn't move, like a crystal, a vase, or a book. Focus your attention on the object, but begin to focus your awareness on your peripheral vision. Take note of the objects surrounding you in your mind. Do you see shadows or sparks of light in your peripheral vision? Make note of what you saw or felt. My fellow Gen Xers may remember the magic posters. Those were the posters that were popular in the late 80s and early 90s. What appeared to be just a poster of patterns actually contained a hidden picture within the poster. You had to almost look through the picture and unfocus your glare in order to see the picture that was hidden within the pattern. These are another great practice for strengthening your clairvoyance ability. Some people who are clairvoyant may even be able to see a person's or thing's aura. An aura is a distinctive atmosphere surrounding a given source. It looks like different colors of light that surround a person or thing. Clairvoyance is often associated with our third eye chakra or 2nd chakra, which is the chakra located in the middle of your forehead.

Another way to strengthen this ability is to work on opening up your third eye chakra. You can do that through guided meditation or again with crystals. The crystals associated with the third eye chakra are sodalite, lapis lazuli, blue kyanite, and azurite. You can meditate with the crystal on your third eye chakra. I find that just holding the crystals while sitting in stillness helps me to connect more.

The last and final form of intuition is clairsentience. This is all about feeling. I also connect very strongly with this form of intuition because I am an empath. An empath is a person with the ability to connect to the mental or emotional state of another individual.

I tend to absorb the feelings and vibes of situations and people around me. How do you know if you are clairsentient? You may have been called "too sensitive." You may feel drained when you are in large crowds and prefer to be alone. You might love being in nature. Maybe you always get gut feelings or have a physiological reaction to certain people or places. Perhaps you often use the phrase "I feel". You know that old saying that the hair on the back of your neck stands up when you meet someone you don't like. That is what this saying is referring to. You have a physiological response in your body when something is off, whether it's a person or a situation.

Clairsentients are often introverts because being in public is downright overwhelming to them. This is a difficult ability to have because it can be very draining, and it is disheartening to know when people lie to you or to know that someone isn't a good person. I can usually tell what someone's true intentions are even before I meet them.

It's not a pleasant thing when you run into shady characters, especially when people you love think those people are wonderful. I remember one time I did a card reading on Facebook. I couldn't really see the people I was reading for. I just saw their Facebook avatar on the screen. I had one person ask me to pull a card for them. As soon as I connected to this person, I felt an overwhelming sense of sorrow and despair. I felt it so intensely that I started crying live on air. That was how strongly I had connected to what the person was feeling, and we weren't even in the same physical space.

It is so important to learn how to shield yourself or turn off the ability to feel other people's emotions when you need to. When you are an empath, it can be easy to take on the energy of everything around you. You don't want to walk around in public and feel overwhelmed all the time. You will need to learn how to protect your energy. It's also important to regularly check in with yourself. When you start to feel sad or any other strong emotion, ask yourself if this is really yours. Oftentimes it is not. It's amazing how much energy you can pick up that is not your own.

After reading this, you may be asking yourself, "Why in the hell would I want to strengthen this ability? It sounds awful." Well, it can be useful, and you can learn to control it. You can learn how to do a shielding exercise to protect your energy. I have one on my YouTube channel. Ask Archangel Michael to surround you in his protective energy. I usually imagine his beautiful blue energy surrounding me like a protective bubble. Do that when you have to be around people. I usually start my day with that. If you do want to strengthen your clairsentient abilities, you can do that by doing the following activity. Ask a friend or family member to show you a picture of someone they know that you do not know. Look at the picture and then try to focus on any feelings that come to you. How was that person feeling in the photo? Pay attention to how you begin to feel. Ask yourself what kind of person this is. Trust what you get and then relay it back to your friend.

There is also another simple exercise you can do to test this ability if you would like to be able to get yes or no answers about people or situations. To do this exercise, simply close your eyes, take a deep breath, and say out loud the word no. Do it over and over again and pay attention to how your body feels. Where do you feel a no in your body? When I do this exercise, I feel a no in my chest. It feels like a tightening in my chest. You can feel it anywhere in your body. Everyone feels it differently. The important thing is to pay attention to how you feel after you hear the word no. You are looking for a physiological reaction in your body. Now you are going to do the same thing only instead of saying no, you will repeat the word yes. Where do you feel a yes in your body? I feel butterflies in my stomach.

Again, it doesn't matter where it shows up for you. The important thing is to pay attention to where you are feeling it in your body. We all have an inner knowing. Our intuition is that inner knowing, and we can use it to guide us in life. Now, when you have important decisions to make, you can check in with yourself. You can ask yourself questions like, "Is this job a good fit for me?" Pay attention to how you feel. Your intuition will not steer you wrong. Clairsentience is also connected to our 2nd chakra or third eye chakra. Another way to strengthen this ability is by doing a guided meditation to open your third eye. There are a lot of ways to open your third eye. You can use crystals, essential oils, and more.

Now, you may be wondering why I went through each of the different forms of intuition. I did this because these are the tools we use when we connect to our crossed over loved ones. When a medium or psychic is giving you information (if they are a genuine psychic), they are using their abilities in one or more of these areas to bring you that information. By strengthening your own abilities, you can receive comforting messages yourself. You don't have to rely on psychics or mediums to feel connected to your loved ones. The more you strengthen your abilities, the better you will be able to communicate with them. Anyone can look up information about you online these days. If you are going to work with a medium, be very careful about whom you select. They should be able to give you information that would not be found online. Look for recommendations and reviews from others. People will leave honest reviews. It's also important not to be too closed off when you work with a medium because that makes your energy harder to connect to.

I mentioned earlier that our loved ones are vibrating at a much higher energetic frequency than we are. That is an important thing to note because it means that we need to raise our energetic vibration in order to more easily connect. You may be asking yourself, "How do I raise my energetic vibration?" Do you think I would honestly tell you that you need to raise your vibration, but not actually demonstrate how to do it? Come on now, you know me better than that. Of course, I am going to tell you how to raise your vibration. There are so many ways you can go about it. The first thing I suggest doing is an energetic clearing. We pick up so much negative energy throughout our day from what we see and hear that it is important to regularly clear your energy. You probably do this with your diet from time to time. You know how it is. You eat so much junk while on vacation. When you get home, you make a promise to eat better. This is no different. You can do a guided meditation to clear your energy, and I even happen to have one on my YouTube channel. You can also just do a search for energy clearing guided meditations on YouTube.

If you want to quickly clear your energy, do the following exercise. Find a quiet place, close your eyes, and imagine a beautiful light (it doesn't matter what color the light is) running from up above going down into the top of your head and down throughout your entire body. Feel that light cleansing you. I almost imagine what it feels like when I step out into the warmth of the sun. Allow that light and warmth to flow all the way down through your body and out through the soles of your feet and into the Earth. Then take a few more deep cleansing breaths, and you are good to go.

Another way to raise your vibration is through music. There are 9 solfeggio frequencies that you can listen to that raise your vibration. Listening to 741 megahertz can help you to open up to your intuition. You can find these on YouTube as well. Isn't YouTube just an amazing source for all things metaphysical? They really need to pay me for the advertisement. I do love that there are so many free tools out there and so many amazing content creators. Go give them some love. Listening to music that is upbeat is a great way to raise your vibration. It doesn't have to be the solfeggio tones. It just needs to be something upbeat that will improve your mood.

Movement is another way to quickly raise your energetic frequency. Go for a walk or go dancing. Besides, dancing is fun and keeps you fit. Another great way to raise your energetic vibration is to do what is called "Earthing." This is where you walk around outside barefoot. As a little girl, I never had shoes on. I hated wearing them. I walked around barefoot everywhere. In fact, at night my feet would be so dirty. Of course, I had to take a bath, and my mom was always in awe of how dirty my feet were. I never realized that I was just Earthing. I loved running in the grass. I loved the way it felt on my feet. Nature is super grounding, and it's a quick and easy way to raise your vibration. Go stand in the sun with your feet in the grass. When you do, really pay attention to how the grass feels on your feet or how the sun feels on your face. It feels amazing.

Water also has many natural healing and cleansing properties. That is why so many people choose to go to the beach to unwind. If you have access to the beach, go and put your feet in the water. If you don't have access, you could listen to the sound of waves crashing on the shore or the sound of a creek. It's amazing how relaxing the sound of water can be. Of course, it can also cause an urge to use the bathroom, so maybe don't drink a lot before you try this. There is always a downside. Speaking of water being healing, you can also take a hot bath in Epsom salt. Drop a few of your favorite essential oils in to help you relax even more. I love lavender. Take a hot bath, listen to relaxing music or the sound of the ocean, dim the lights or light a candle, and just allow all of your worries to melt away.

Avoiding negativity is one of the best ways to ensure that your vibration stays elevated. I know…you just said to yourself," How am I supposed to avoid negativity? The world is full of assholes." You're not wrong, I mean there are still some awesome people left in this world, but I understand how you feel. There are some things you can do to avoid negativity. You have to learn to say no to things that don't bring you joy. That's a tough lesson. As a reformed people pleaser, I wanted to make everyone happy.

The only problem with that is you end up being the person not happy when you do that. Learn to set boundaries for yourself. Say no when something doesn't feel like a soul yes.My first book Beautifully Broken has a great chapter on setting boundaries if you need some help with this. Make time to do things that bring you joy. Create something, go get a massage, go have a fun visit with friends. Anything that you can do to make yourself feel better (not unnaturally like drugs) is going to raise your vibration.

One of the best ways to raise your vibration is through gratitude. When we are grateful for what we have, we feel good. It also signals to the Universe that we want more of that good stuff. Like attracts like, so try to keep your mindset positive. Find 5 things right now that you are grateful for. I'm so grateful for my kids, my family, my dogs, my friends, those of you who bought this book, and so much more. The more things you find to be grateful for, the more you will see all the beautiful things around you. Think about it this way…how do you feel when you give someone a gift, and you know that they are truly thankful for it? It feels good, right? Now think about how you feel when you give someone a gift, and you can tell they didn't like it or appreciate it. You don't ever want to give them a gift again because man are they demanding and ungrateful. I will never forget when my son was three. A family friend gave him clothes for his birthday. He marched right over to me and said, "I do not appreciate clothing." Say that in your sassiest three-year-old voice because that's exactly what it sounded like.

I wanted to die right there. I was sure that they had heard him. I ever so politely pulled him by the arm and whispered through my clenched teeth. You say thank you like you like it. Aww, kids. They're great, right? My point is that the Universe loves when we appreciate all that we have. The more we appreciate what we have and where we are right now…even if it isn't where we want to be yet…the more we attract amazing things to love.

Earlier I mentioned that crystals can help to strengthen and clear some of your chakras. They can also help you to raise your vibration and clear your energy. I love working with black obsidian, amethyst, and clear quartz crystals. I think they are so powerful. Go to a shop that sells them and pick out the ones you like. You can also order them online, just make sure you read the reviews and ensure that the seller is reputable. I really like going to shop for crystals. I want to be able to pick the crystal up and hold it before I buy it. I can personally feel their energy when I pick up different crystals.

They're pretty to look at, and they can improve your mood too. Selenite and blue kyanite are other crystals that I really like using. I just sit in stillness and hold them for a few minutes with my eyes closed. I set the intention that I am clearing my energy and raising my vibration. You can hold them when you meditate too or put them on certain points of the body. If you would like more information about crystals. I recorded an episode about them on my podcast Awaken Your Inner Awesomeness .

Once you have raised your vibration, and you have worked on strengthening your intuitive abilities, you can begin trying to connect to your departed loved one. The easiest way to connect is to ask for signs. Loved ones will often leave objects in our paths. Coins, feathers, and heart shaped things are the most common objects that people find. Ask for something specific. You could say, "Show me cardinals when you are around." Maybe you ask for them to play you a specific song. Maybe you would like to hear their voice or even feel their essence around you. You can ask for that too. When my grandpa was around me, I would smell cigarette smoke. I never met him, and one of the few things I really knew about him was that he smoked. I would be in the car by myself and suddenly smell cigarette smoke. I also felt a tingling on the back of my head like someone was touching my hair. It was the craziest feeling, but I knew it had to be him. As I mentioned earlier, I got a reading years later, and I was told that he was always around my daughter and I to protect us. It made total sense to me. Besides, I already knew he was there.

Your loved ones can come through in so many ways. You can ask for specific ways, or you can just put out the intention that you wish to connect to them and see what happens. I will sometimes see shadows out of the corner of my eyes. When I do, I know that my loved ones are there. You can talk to them. They hear you. Say whatever it is that you would like to say. Pay attention to how you feel when you do talk to them. Sometimes I feel a tingling on my cheek. I know that is my mom giving me a kiss. Again, the way you connect may be different. We all have unique stories. You may have vivid visitation dreams, or you may have animals that seem to find you. I dream about my mom a lot. Sometimes the dreams feel so real that I don't want to wake up. She talks and talks to me in these dreams. I don't always remember everything she said, but it always feels like we had a big heart-to-heart conversation when I wake up. You may want to keep a dream journal by your bed. That way when you wake up, you can write down what you remember about your dream so that you do not forget it. However, you choose to connect, it's a comfort to know and have proof that our loved ones never really leave us. They are always trying to get our attention and let us know that they are around. We just have to be open and pay attention to the signs they give us. It's an honor to be able to get visitations from them, and they can still be very much connected to you in your daily life.

CHAPTER 12
HOW QUICKLY EVERYTHING CHANGES

They say that grief changes you, and I absolutely believe that this is one hundred percent true. I know that I am not the same person that I was before my mom got sick. The interesting thing about experiencing change is that one can react to it in a myriad of ways. You can learn how to adapt and begin to heal, or you can avoid it and begin to self-destruct. You can also be somewhere in the middle of those two extremes. I knew my life would be quite different without my mom. She was a huge part of it, after all. What I didn't realize was just how quickly everything in my life would change after her death. My whole family dynamic changed. I was no longer close with many of my family members and friends because my mom was the glue that held us all together. Without her, we were all lost. I also believe that in part it is because we all have different needs and grieve in different ways. Some people need to rely on others for support when they grieve, while others want to be alone.

The fascinating thing about change is that as humans, we fear it immensely. We tend to hold onto what is comfortable. As we know, all circumstances in life must change. It is just a part of the natural evolution of things. After my mom's death, some aspects of my life changed for the better, while other things not so much. The most noticeable change for me was in the relationships with certain people in my life. Some of the people that I was the closest to became very distant after my mom's passing. My brother was really one of the biggest examples of this. I wasn't the only one that he pushed away, but we lived together and were always very close, so it was most obvious to me that he was drawing away from the family. The first year after my mom's death was so difficult for me because I wasn't just grieving my mom's death. I was also grieving the loss of our entire family dynamic. My mom was the reason we were so close. We would go to her house or out to eat with her often. When she passed away, my kids weren't around because they were in college, and the friendship that I had with my brother became very strained.

At first, my brother and I leaned on each other after her passing. We did a lot of things together the summer after she died. We had season tickets to the Cardinals baseball games and even took a road trip to Milwaukee to see them play. I noticed even then that when we were hanging out together, something was a little off with him. He never wanted to talk about my mom and would only do so on rare occasions. I worried about him because it didn't seem like he was dealing with his grief. He seemed to be avoiding it at all costs. That is a very normal coping mechanism, but it is also extremely unhealthy.

After that summer, he started growing increasingly distant. We would make family plans, but he didn't join us. This wasn't like my brother. He had always loved being around family. I think that being with us reminded him too much of my mom's absence. It was really difficult for him because he was very close to my mom. Towards the end of her life, my brother really never left her side. It breaks my heart as I'm writing this to think about that. I didn't understand at the time what my brother was truly going through. I couldn't see how much pain he was really in. I just saw that he would flake out on us when we would try to make plans, which caused me pain. He became a stranger to us. It hurt me a lot because I didn't understand why he was acting this way. It's only now, after I have had my own grief counseling sessions, that I realize he was simply trying to grieve in his own way. Unfortunately, this caused some tension between my brother and I.

I never expected to feel that way about him. I love my brother very much. I know he would never want to hurt me on purpose. Our relationship was rocky when we were younger because I was his bratty little sister. I annoyed him every waking moment. We never got along as kids, and we fought all the time because you know, "All I wanted was one brother, and instead I got two sisters." It wasn't until he went off to college that our relationship began to change. After I graduated from college, we really bonded. We traveled to Europe together and even worked for the same company for a little while. We had always had a close relationship since that time. He was there for me after my divorce. He let my kids and me move in with him. Several years later, I bought a house, and he moved in with us. We've always had each other's backs no matter what. That all changed after my mom died. At that time, it felt like he just disappeared, and I didn't know where he went. I knew where he was there physically, but emotionally and mentally, he was checked out. I'm happy to report that we have been able to reconnect these past few months. Counseling, time, and patience have made a major impact for the better for both of us. Again, I think that processing my mom's death played a huge role in why we drifted apart in the first place.

So, at 45 years old, I was now living alone. I had never really lived alone before. Now, my kids were off at college, and it was just my dogs and me. On top of figuring out how to get on with my life without my mom, I also had to figure out how to be alone and do things I have never done before, like mowing the grass. The worst part was having a huge hole in my life where my brother once was. This was a huge loss for me. It is so hard to have to grieve for someone who is still living. It is especially difficult when everyone else sees that this person has changed, but they don't see it themselves. The worst feeling in the world is to have to stand by and watch someone you love become someone you don't even recognize.

It pained me to know that he was hurting and needed help, but there was nothing I could do for him. I couldn't force him to go get help. Talking to him one-on-one and recommending counseling didn't do anything to help. So, I just waited and prayed that God would intervene on his behalf. I prayed that he would choose to face his grief head on and learn to heal from it. That was all I could do, and even though it felt extremely helpless, it's what I did. I'm happy to say that my prayers seem to be working. I have been able to spend a lot more time with him lately, and I have enjoyed having my brother back in my life.

Although that particular relationship waned, other relationships in my life actually deepened after my mom's passing. My sister and I became even closer than we already were. We both make sure we text each other and ask if the other is doing OK. We also make sure to get together regularly. She and I talk quite a bit and have even gone to grief counseling together. I have really appreciated her support and wisdom. Her grief isn't the same as mine, but it's comforting to know that I can talk to her whenever I need someone. She is always there. My brother-in-law has also been equally supportive. Luckily, I have friends and other family who also reach out and send loving messages of support. It really does help to know that others still care. After a loved one dies, most people share their sympathy and then forget about you. It's not that they mean to be cruel. Life gets busy, and we forget to check on those who may need it most.

My relationship with my kids has also grown. Even though they are both busy and my daughter moved away for school, I see them and how they are growing and maturing. I get to spend quality time with them. The time I have with them is so much richer because I appreciate it much more now than I did before. I think they do too. We have all unfortunately learned how precious life is. We are never guaranteed even one single second on this earth. It has also made me reflect on what kind of mom I want to be for my kids. I know that I wasn't perfect when my kids were growing up. As a single mom, I was often impatient and exhausted. That isn't how I want my kids to view me now. I want them to know that I am always here for them, and I want us to be close.

One of the hardest lessons that we come here to learn is about unconditional love. We came here to learn how to love others unconditionally, which means that we must learn to love people even at their worst. This is not an easy concept. It can hurt when people do things to hurt you whether it's intentional or not. You can still love that person. Sometimes you just have to do it at a distance. Sometimes all you can do is love people where they are. That is why this time has been so incredibly challenging for me. I love my brother and always will. I will always be here for him, too, but there was a fine line between loving him and allowing him to hurt me. For a time, I had to love him at a distance.

I had to give him his space. I hoped that one day when he was ready, he would come back around, be ready to heal, and be a part of our family again. I knew we would be ready to welcome him in with open arms when he did. That is exactly what happened. We held space for him, and when he was ready, he did eventually come back.

My mom's passing has changed my outlook on life in general. I try not to sweat the small stuff too much anymore because I know that at the end of my life, those things will not have mattered in the slightest. It's easy to feel like you are a victim in life, but that really doesn't accomplish much for you. Believe me when I say that I played the victim role all too well. The problem is that when you are a victim, you are playing a very passive role in your life. When you understand that your attitude, thoughts, and actions play the biggest part in your life, you begin to understand what truly counts. If you want to experience better things in life, you have to make that happen. No one else can do that for you. That is why being fully present in your life is so critical.

After my mom's passing, I decided that I wanted to try more things. I went on my first cruise ever with my family, and the next year we all went to Italy and Greece. Greece was a bucket list item for me. I think that is what is truly important. Living life and experiencing all the things while you are here. If I had decided to stop living after my mom died, then I wouldn't be doing these things. I had to prove to myself that I am resilient and can survive what may seem like insurmountable challenges. I know that you are a strong and resilient person too. You will get through this. You have many more exciting adventures awaiting you if you choose to participate in life again.

It's true that the relationships I had with certain people in my life have drastically changed. While it did make me sad, and I grieved for that loss too, I also had to come to terms with my reality. I could sit and wallow in my sorrow, or I could choose to go on and make new connections. I know which choice felt better for me. If your family dynamic changed like mine, then I sympathize with you. I know it is difficult and painful. Death often leads to a disintegration of the family when the one who died was the glue that held it together. You do need to acknowledge your feelings; however, residing in that place of despair will not create any positive changes. Some things are simply out of our control. Life circumstances happen, and we can be left feeling lost. Revisit the chapter on rebuilding your life. That advice can work for building new friendships too. You will meet new people, and you will have so many adventures if you dare to dream it.

CHAPTER 13

GRIEF: THE GREATEST TEACHER I NEVER EXPECTED

One of the biggest questions we ask ourselves after a loved one passes is, "Why?" I know I asked myself the following questions over and over again. Why did I have to lose my mom? Why did this happen to me? Why did she have to die so young? Why did she have to suffer? Why do I have to live the rest of my life without her? Why do horrible people live to be ancient, while wonderful people die young? Those questions and others ran in a loop through my brain. It is so very difficult for our hearts and minds to understand loss. Death creates a huge void that we end up filling with all of these questions. One question leads to a million others, and soon you've gone down a rabbit hole of questioning everything. The problem with this is that these questions are not productive. They don't bring back our loved ones or help us understand anything. They simply drive us crazy. They become intrusive thoughts that keep us awake at night and keep us in a mental prison.

Whenever I start going down the rabbit hole of questions, I have to physically stop myself. These questions aren't going to bring me closure, but I realize that there is a reason I am asking them. That reason is that my brain is trying to process what just happened. One minute my loved one was here, and the next they were gone. It feels like a nightmare that I can't wake up from. Sometimes when we dream, we are receiving messages from our unconscious mind. Sometimes those messages give us the answers we are seeking. Just like in our dreams, there are messages, or rather lessons in grief. We don't experience loss without a reason. It is here to teach us. Therefore, an important task for us once we experience loss is to uncover what those lessons are. Only then will we truly begin to process our grief and get a clear understanding of it.

It is my belief that before we ever come to this school we call Earth, we choose lessons that we want to learn. We learn these particular lessons through experiences we have while here. For example, if we want to learn patience, we have to go through something that teaches us patience. We may experience a brief illness that causes us to slow down in life. If we want to learn about unconditional love, we have to go through situations that teach us about unconditional love. We may be put with family members who are tough to love. We may have to learn to love them as they are. Maybe we even learn to set boundaries with our family, so we learn self-love as well. There are so many reasons we choose to come here, and we have so many different lessons that we are supposed to learn while we are here.

I know you must be saying to yourself right now, "I would never have chosen to experience this kind of pain. There is no way that I chose this lesson for myself." Believe me, I understand how you feel. It is incomprehensible that we would actually want to go through all the tough times that we do. Let me clarify what I mean with this example. If you went to college or high school, you were able to pick your courses. You had a course guide in front of you that described the classes. You didn't know what it would actually be like once you got there. You simply had to rely on the descriptions. When I first went to college, I was so excited to pick out my classes. I had my course guide in front of me to help me make my selections. I read each one excitedly. They made every class sound so amazing. Underwater basket weaving - create the basket of your dreams while swimming underwater with mermaids. I mean, the imagery alone was enough to entice me. I may be exaggerating just a bit; however, this is exactly how I was tricked into taking philosophy. It sounded so interesting and mature. I was in college, after all. I wanted to look and feel like a grownup. I was so excited to take this course that I actually wore glasses to class, even though I didn't need them. I wanted to appear smarter than I truly was. That was quite a task. When the first day arrived, and I actually went to class, I realized immediately that I had made a huge mistake. How could something that sounded so thrilling be so boring and useless? I don't know how, but it was. My apologies to any philosophy professors out there. I suffered all semester through that class. The two hours that class lasted each day felt like seven years. I couldn't wait for the semester to end.

My point is this–just like in school, we pick lessons like classes. The goal is to choose lessons that teach us a lot in a short time span. The goal is to elevate our souls as quickly as possible. Before we came here, we chose extremely difficult lessons because that is the fastest way to learn and grow. When we are on the other side, we don't remember how hard and painful those lessons can be. On the other side, everything is beautiful and blissful.

Everything is unconditional love and peace. We forget what an armpit Earth can be. We're all happy and living joyfully when we pick our lessons. That is why we pick underwater basket weaving or philosophy. It sounds cool and interesting, and we will learn a lot. What we don't realize is that when we get here and experience it, we will curse our higher selves for picking it. I have seen videos of spiritual teachers on TikTok who say things like, "You should be honored that your soul chose to come to Earth because it's one of the hardest schools." Really? You think? Thank you, Captain Obvious! Anyone who breathes air out of their lungs knows that just existing here on Earth is excruciating. In fact, everyone comes here with built-in trauma because just being birthed is traumatic. Most of the responses in the comments of those videos are hilarious. People write things like, "Did this come with a 90-day money-back guarantee?" Or they say, "I'd like to cancel my subscription. Not a fan. Can I just go home?" Everyone thinks it's difficult to be here. You are not alone, but you should feel honored. You are surviving one of the hardest places to learn. It's like going to Princeton, Harvard, or Yale for your soul.

The reason that I mention that we came here to learn is because this terrible thing you've experienced, this grief, is teaching you something. You chose to experience this in order for your soul to learn, grow, and elevate. I know you're talking back to me right now and saying that you definitely did not pick this, but I am telling you that you did. We pick our lessons. I don't believe that God, our Higher Power, or whatever you want to call It, sits up there somewhere laughing at our misery saying things like,

"Watch what happens when I throw this at them. Those poor idiots." I know it feels like this is what happens, but it isn't. If you are a parent, think about the experiences you had with your own children. You wanted to protect them, but they had to learn things on their own too. It's no different in this situation. We have to be put through some painful tests in order to learn things. We make soul agreements with other souls to come here to learn, and it is our job to complete the assignment. You even made an agreement with that asshole ex of yours to come here and experience your relationship. On the other side, you were probably friends or part of the same soul family. You said, "Wouldn't it be fun to come here at the same time and work through this lesson by torturing each other?" It was super fun...right? The fun just never stops.

I know that all of this sounds so improbable. Our human brains have a really hard time digesting this information. Plus, traditional religion does not teach us anything about this. Traditional religion would have us believe that we deserve the bad things that happen to us, or that God is up there just throwing horrible scenarios our way. That is not true at all. What I know to be true is that learning is just one of the many missions of our soul. In fact, our souls look for opportunities to learn, so if you make a mistake and feel stupid about it, just tell yourself that you are not, in fact, a total idiot. Your soul just needed an opportunity to learn. Now, don't you feel better? You're welcome.

My mom's passing taught me a great deal. I have grown more in the past few years than in my entire life. If you think you feel self-sufficient and strong, try losing a parent. That changes your attitude really quickly. I went from feeling like I could handle anything to thinking, "Now what do I do? I don't even have a mom anymore." It can be really tough. Look at it this way, if your life was blissful all the time, then what is there to learn? I mean, sure...your life is wonderful. Maybe you learn how to live on a yacht...why is that bad again? Oh yes, because it's not in times of abundance, happiness, and peace that we learn. We learn through struggle. When we are at our lowest point in life, we learn how strong and resilient we are. We learn how to ask for help, and we learn so many other things. I know that I learned a great deal these past two years. Some of the lessons that I have learned have been about patience, selfishness, and empathy.

I remember when my mom was very sick. This was a few weeks before her death. Oddly enough, right at this time everyone who had been helping us take care of her during her illness became unavailable for one reason or another. One of our friends got Covid, my sister went out of town, and other friends were out of town too. Additionally, we didn't realize that she was so close to death. It was just my brother and I left to take care of her, and she was getting sicker and sicker and required a lot more care. Her needs grew exponentially within a matter of days, and she reverted almost to a childlike state. She had to be fed and helped to the bathroom. It was difficult for her to do anything for herself because she was so weak. In fact, it reminded me of taking care of my kids when they were little. She required the same demand of my time and energy. She couldn't walk by herself because she had become so unsteady. There were times when I became very frustrated with her because I felt like she wasn't helping herself enough. I feel bad thinking about it now, but at the time I felt like she was giving up when she could have fought harder. Little did I know that she was actively dying. She just got weaker and weaker. It required patience from me to take care of her, but I also had to have patience with myself. I was doing the best that I could. After all, I had never taken care of someone who was so sick before. I had to learn not to get frustrated and instead to have more compassion. She and I were in this thing together.

One particularly bad night, she got up to go to the bathroom around midnight. She was so stubborn (I'm getting the look now. I can feel it) that she refused to use a walker to help stabilize her when she was walking. We tried and tried to convince her to use it, but she wouldn't. She preferred to lean on whoever was leading her. I was walking with her back to our living room. She had been staying at my home. She became unsteady and grabbed my arm, which threw my balance off too because I was half asleep. She started falling. I tried to catch her, but I couldn't hold her up. Although she only weighed about 100 pounds, if that, it was dead weight and too much for me to hold. We both fell, and I just knew that I had hurt her. We were both crying. I was terrified. She landed in such a mangled way that I knew I had broken her legs. I was screaming for help, but my brother couldn't hear me because his room was in the basement. It was all I could do to pull her up into a sitting position and drag her to the wall to prop her up until I could get help. Thankfully, she wasn't hurt. It just scared us both. I will not soon forget that night. I cried myself to sleep after we got her back in bed because I knew this was the beginning of the end for us. I was scared about what we were going to do. I knew this was too much for my brother and me to handle. It was exhausting, but I am so glad we were able to do it. I would never have wanted to put her in a facility, but I completely understand why people have to do that.

It's really tough caring for someone who needs a lot of medical attention. Luckily, my aunt Connie offered to let my mom come and stay with her. She had a hospital bed and could be there around the clock with her. She also had experience taking care of people with a lot of medical needs. We were so thankful for her because it lifted so much of the stress from us.

A few weeks before that incident, my brother and I were at my mom's house getting her ready for bed. That's how quickly she became unable to stay by herself. Just a matter of weeks and she would be unable to care for herself. That night it was just the two of us with her. I had to help her into bed because she no longer had enough strength to pull herself up onto her bed. I think she knew that her time was running out. She was sicker than she had let any of us know. Nighttimes were the hardest for her, and I think one reason is that she feared she would die in her sleep and would be alone when she passed. It's gut-wrenching to think of that now. As humans, we fear the unknown. That was one of her biggest fears, to be alone. You learn a lot about empathy and kindness when you care for someone who is sick. I had to check my own attitude sometimes because I had no idea what my mom was going through. It is easy to lose patience with someone when you are responsible for their every need. It can be downright exhausting. The worst part is that when I would start to feel frustrated, she would look up at me with childlike innocence and say, "I'm sorry." That ripped my heart out. In fact, the last few months of her life she uttered "I'm sorry" so often that I began to hate those words. They tugged at my heartstrings every single time. It's so important to be kind. She was afraid of dying, and I completely understand why. Luckily, I have since learned through my interviews with many people who have experienced near death that death is nothing to fear. We are never alone, and the other side is a judgment-free and loving place.

This particular night, my mom said she was scared, and she started to get weepy. I crawled into bed with her and held her. I told her every little thing was going to be alright. When she was first diagnosed with cancer, we would sing that Bob Marley song to each other. It held a special meaning for us because we knew it meant that no matter what happened, whether she lived or if she went home to be with God, she would be OK. She then got quiet and whispered that she missed her mom, and she began to silently sob. My grandma had passed away just the year before. My mom was her main caretaker and was very close to her. My grandma used to say that my mom was her right arm. It was a tough time to lose her because it was during Covid, and my mom was deep in her own battle with cancer.I was very close to my mom, and I feared that she might just give up because she wanted to go and be with her mom.

Losing my mom was one of my greatest fears and had been since I was that little 7-year-old girl who prayed for her safety. I said to her, "I know how you feel. I would feel the same way if anything happened to you." I then told her a story. My parents divorced when I was three. My dad would come and get us every other weekend. I love my dad, but I always felt a little out of sorts when I had to go to his house on the weekends. It wasn't because of anything he did. He loved us and took excellent care of us. It was simply because I missed my room, my mom, and my friends. I also missed my routine at home. I like structure. I'm the girl who lays out my clothes the night before work. Any kind of change was difficult for me.

My dad would come get us after work on Friday and bring us home on Sunday. His aunt (my great aunt Gee) lived next door to my mom. He would bring us to her house, and she always had a delicious dessert of some kind waiting. My dad would go in and have a slice of pie and visit with her. My mom would often come over and visit too. I would be so happy to see her. I would crawl in her lap and lay my head on her chest. I could hear her heartbeat, and it made me feel safe. As a little girl, I would sometimes be unable to fall asleep at night. I would go ask my mom if I could sleep with her. She always said yes, even though I know she would have preferred to have the whole bed to herself. I would hug her and again hear her heartbeat, and I would be able to sleep immediately. There was something safe about hearing that sound. I had never told her this before, and when I finished telling her this story, she began sobbing even harder. My brother walked in, saw us sobbing, and he began to cry as well. We both told her how much we loved her and that she needed to keep fighting, but we both had a sinking feeling. We again tried to reassure her that every little thing would be alright.

I am so glad that I had the opportunity to spend that time with my mom. I'm especially glad that I told her how I felt. I know it was tough for her as a single mom. I know she got frustrated with us, and she often felt unappreciated. I also know that later in life, she worried that she didn't do enough for us when we were kids. We reassured her that she did. I believe that as a parent, you always worry that you could or should have done more for your kids. I know that is how I felt as a single mom. Being a single mom is one of the most challenging experiences there is. So, to be able to tell her how much she meant to me and to be able to hold her and be the one to make her feel safe is priceless.

Taking care of my mom required a lot of patience because at the time, I didn't understand how bad she really was. I know that seems stupid to say. I know she had pancreatic cancer, but the doctors were not really explaining anything. It was as if they didn't know what was going to happen to her either. Plus, we quickly went from thinking she's cancer free to facing the fact that it's back and there's not much we can do.

It's actually mind-boggling how quickly things shifted. One minute we were posting videos of her ringing a bell, and the next we were asking for prayers because she was clinging to life. We fought and fought for my mom, but at some point we had to make the tough decision to let her go. Having to make that judgment call was excruciating. I heard a hospice nurse speak about this topic not very long ago. She said she is horrified when families try to keep fighting for their loved one when they are actively dying. It only prolongs their loved one's suffering. I felt a jolt of pain right through the heart when I heard that because I knew that we had inadvertently done that to my mom. The nurse said that she blamed many of the doctors. Doctors do not want to be the ones to give bad news, so they try to pass families off to hospice and let the hospice nurses do it. That's how we felt. We felt blindsided by what happened at the end, and we were totally unprepared, but I can pinpoint exactly when she got worse. It was right after she had her last round of chemo. That last dose of poison did it for her. If I could do anything differently, it would be to have made sure the end of her life was more comfortable than it was. I would have let her eat all the junk food she wanted. I wouldn't have lost my patience with her. I would have just sat with her and asked her about her life. Those are the things that matter most in the end.

Kindness and empathy are big lessons, but neither was as tough as the one that was waiting ahead for us. One of the toughest lessons my siblings and I had to learn was in selflessness. We had to learn to let go of our need to hold onto our mom. As much as we loved her, needed her, and would miss her, to see her suffering was unbearable. She spent her life devoted to taking care of us, and now it was time for us to care for her. As is a common occurrence when a loved one is dying, my mom clung to life until one by one we went in, told her everything we needed to say to her, and let her know that it was ok for her to go. I know she was listening, She wanted to know that we would be fine without her. We each held her hand, and she was surrounded by love as she took her final breath. Her fear of dying alone was thankfully never realized.

If you are afraid of dying alone, let me ease your fears. It's my belief that even when a person does die alone, they are never truly alone. There is a team of angels and departed loved ones that come and surround them and wait to take them home. Many people often hear their loved ones talking about angels and departed family members even before they die. Every person that I have interviewed about near-death experiences tells me that they feel immense love, joy, and peace when they are on the other side. May that be a comfort to you.

Grief is a powerful teacher, and there are so many lessons for us to learn. One of the most meaningful lessons is learning to live in the present moment, never taking anything for granted, and appreciating the value of people and experiences.

Before we lose someone we love, we may take their presence for granted. We take a lot of things for granted. We place value on objects instead of what truly matters. We don't really appreciate the little things in life…shared laughter, warm hugs, profound advice, being present. There is so much for us to cherish. What is most valuable becomes glaringly obvious after it is gone. Never in my wildest dreams did I imagine having to live from the age of 45 on without my mom. It seems incomprehensible and inconceivable. The only thing that comforts me is that she left me with so many gifts. I teach German, and one of the quirky little things that I love about the language is how the people use certain words to lovingly refer to the people in their lives that they care about the most. They like to use the word Schatz or Schatzi, which means treasure. I absolutely adore that because it's the people and moments in our lives that are a true treasure, not material possessions. When the things are gone, they're gone. When our loved ones pass, they leave with us a legacy of beautiful memories to keep and cherish.

I read a quote the other day that says the things we lose have a way of coming back to us. While they don't physically come back to us, they do return in a number of ways...from shared memories, future children, and even in our own personal attributes that were shaped and molded by our loved ones. I can't tell you how many times since my mom passed we think of her. When someone says something stupid, we all say in unison, "Mom would be crossing her eyes right now." We all know the look she would be giving whoever was making an idiotic comment. Some of us can even replicate that look. We were taught by the best. As long as we remember her, her spirit is still very much alive and a part of our lives.

My mom was a true teacher in life even until the very end. Her death taught us so many things whether it was to appreciate life, live in the moment, or to value the people in your life. You never know how long you have here. She always used to say that you are never promised even one second on this Earth. She was absolutely correct. We should start living as if that is our truth. Be adventurous, laugh often, love hard because in the end, that is all that really matters anyway. The love you created is the love you take. So, grief was a teacher that I never expected to show up in my life, but I can certainly appreciate the lessons it taught me. I choose to remember those lessons as I live my life. You can choose to learn, grow, live, laugh, love, or you can choose to stay stuck, angry, bitter or worse. I know which option feels better. Life is what you make it. You can choose to sit it out, or you can choose to dance. The choice is always yours.

What lesson did your grief teach you? I challenge you today to look at grief as a teacher. Yes, grief is a hard-nosed, strict, and often tough teacher. Those are the teachers who taught you the most anyway.

You don't always have to like your teacher to learn from him or her. Maybe you don't like grief, but it is teaching you something. What are you learning from this experience? I challenge you to sit with yourself and do some journaling work. Find a quiet place, set aside some time, and ask yourself the following questions:

- What do I know now that I did not know before my loved one died?

- Is there anything I would do differently now that my loved one has died?

- What would I change in my life now that I have learned to appreciate that tomorrow is not guaranteed?

- Is there anything that I am currently not doing in my life that I would like to start doing more of?

- Is there anything that I am doing in my life that I would like to do less of?

- What would my perfect day look like? ● What brings me joy and happiness?

The answers to these questions will help you to see that death teaches us so many things. We learn to value what is important and let go of what is not. I don't know of anyone who likes grief. It's a nasty thing, but we experience it for a reason. It forces us to learn and grow. It's a natural part of life, and it isn't going anywhere anytime soon. We all have to take the journey. Why not let it be your greatest teacher? What doesn't kill us makes us stronger. I truly believe that. Allow your grief to give you strength and wisdom. Keep the lessons and try as much as it is possible to let the pain go. It won't happen overnight, but it will happen. You can get through it little by little. Grief changes you, but I believe it can change you for the better if you let it.

CHAPTER 14
SIFTING THROUGH THE SADNESS TO FIND YOUR INNER STRENGTH

Grief is one of the most painful experiences that we go through as humans. They say that you never know how strong you really are until you are tested. I believe that through great pain comes great strength. I have certainly found this to be true in my own life. Our mere existence here can be so overwhelming, and we don't always understand why we have to go through so many difficult experiences. One thing I know to be true is that there is always an opportunity to create beauty from devastation. Like a Phoenix who rises from the ashes, we, too, must learn to pick ourselves back up and make something beautiful with the rest of this thing we call life. Yes, you were dealt a bad hand. Unfortunately, there is no one who is exempt from struggle. As Oprah Winfrey once said, "When there is no struggle, there is no strength." Even people who seem to have the perfect life have to go through challenges. That is how we learn, and that's what we came here to do. We came here to learn. The important thing to remember is that one bad chapter does not equal a bad book. Tomorrow is a new day, and you can always turn the page and start a new chapter. It takes strength and courage to move on in life after a deep loss. The thing is that you have to go on living. You don't really have a choice in that, so now it's important that you find that inner strength in order to do just that.

Grief can feel like a tidal wave or some other destructive force of nature. As with any natural disaster, after the dust settles, people gather to figure out how they will rebuild. Usually a community works together to restore what was destroyed. As a German teacher, one of the interesting things that I teach is how cities responded to reconstruction after World War II. The cities had a choice to either restore their buildings to their original splendor, or they could demolish everything and start over. Most cities decided to restore their buildings to their former glory. A few cities decided to demolish the rubble and start over. They did, however, choose to preserve a small part of their city as a reminder of pre-war times. It is fascinating to see the stark contrast. What is worth noting, though, is that in all of those examples, not one of those towns voted to leave the rubble, shut the city down, and give up completely. That would be ridiculous. In the same way, you can't give up either. I know you may want to, but that is not the answer. It's time to rebuild your life. Why not do that with a sense of purpose? While it takes tremendous bravery to start over, it is always worth it in the end. You should never be afraid of falling apart because it presents a wonderful opportunity to rebuild. You can either choose to be a better version of you, or you can be something completely new. Whatever you choose is perfect for you. You can rebrand yourself. Doesn't that sound exciting?

Whenever I go through difficult times in life, I always take a step back and ask myself these questions: "What am I learning?" and "What is this showing me?" I do not believe that we endure pain simply for the sake of feeling pain. Pain always has a purpose. It teaches us something. It isn't always easy to understand what that is at first. We must work on figuring that out for ourselves. For example, one thing I learned after experiencing loss was how to ask others for help. Maybe now that your loved one has passed, you need to rely on others more too. There is no shame in that. Knowing you need help, and asking for it, takes a great deal of courage that most people don't possess. Another big lesson for me has been about fear. I used to worry and have anxiety over everything. Now, I realize that I need to let go of fear. I can't control everything in my life, and trying to do so simply causes mental and emotional stress. It doesn't change anything. I had to learn to stop worrying so much about every little detail of life. I also learned a great deal about strength. It takes a lot of strength and courage to heal from trauma. Most people do not even want to face their traumas, let alone heal them. Losing someone you love is extremely traumatic. I think you are so courageous and brave for wanting to heal. Healing is a very difficult journey, but it is one of the most rewarding journeys there is.

It takes strength to move on after the loss of someone important. It is never easy to move on or to start over in life. Those who dare to make big changes in life are so brave because it takes a lot of courage to do something different. Many of us learn just how strong we are when we are put to the test. After I divorced my ex, I wasn't sure how I was going to make a living or raise two kids on my own. I ended up going back to school to get my teaching degree. I had a degree already, but it was in finance, and I wasn't happy in that field. I knew that this new beginning was a chance for me to redefine who I was in life. It was a chance for me to be who I wanted to be and do what I wanted to do. It wasn't easy, but it paid off in the end.

One of my podcast listeners sent me a song called "Wonder Woman" by Miley Cyrus. She said, "This is you. You are a wonder woman." I felt incredibly humbled because I didn't realize that others saw me this way. I just knew that I didn't have a choice in life. I had to pick up the pieces and move on for my children. The lyrics are, "You never know that she is broken. Cause she's always fine. She's a million moments. Lived a thousand lives." This song describes a lot of women that I know. It takes so much strength to pick yourself back up again after a tragedy. If you are doing that, then you are amazing too. Not everyone heals themselves after a trauma. Most people continue living and bleeding all over people who didn't cut them. I realized that I had a choice. I could give up and keep doing things the way that I had always done them, which didn't produce great results, or I could start over.

As a familiar expression says, "If you don't like something, change it." There is something so exciting about change. I had a choice to make, and I chose not to be a victim. I chose not to stay down when I fell. Yes, a few bad things have happened to me. Everyone experiences hardships in one form or another. It's what we do with that struggle that matters. As Deepak Chopra said, "All great changes are preceded by chaos." It's in that chaos that we truly find ourselves. We can become overwhelmed by it, or we have the opportunity to use our pain to create something beautiful from it.

That is exactly what I chose to do. After each trauma in my life, I have chosen to heal. Following my divorce from my ex, I decided to go on my own healing journey. It wasn't a quick trip. It has taken me, and still takes me, time to heal from everything that cut me. On this journey, I am learning how to love myself, how to set boundaries for myself, and how to take better care of myself. I am also learning how important it is to help others heal. I discovered on this journey that I could use my voice to help those who are in pain. That is why I decided to write my first book *Beautifully Broken*. I found a purpose in my pain. That purpose was helping other women just like me heal. I remember when my mom was sick she said, "Maybe I should write about my experience." I told her that she should because perhaps what she was going through would help someone else. Sadly for us, she only wrote a few paragraphs and never continued to write. It was unfortunate that at the time she decided she should write, her health soon took a downward turn.

What she didn't realize is that she is still helping others. She is helping them through this very book. Pain is not futile if we can find a way to repurpose it. In the same way, our loved ones never die in vain if we hold on to what they taught us. No one can ever be forgotten if we remember what they represented to us. I love this quote by Jack Thorne. He said, "Those we love never truly leave us. There are some things that death cannot touch." What I think he means by this is that death can't steal the memories and the lessons that our loved ones left behind. Death can't rob us of the love we had for those we lost. The legacy that was my mom lives on through her kids and grandkids and the work that we are doing now with this book.

One thing I know about my mom is that she was incredibly proud of all of her kids and grandchildren, and she was proud of everything she accomplished in life. She was a wonder woman too. She was the first person in her family to graduate from college. She raised three kids as a single mom while going back to school. She performed in many local festivals and won many singing contests. She also earned several teaching awards throughout her years as an educator. She set a beautiful example of what picking yourself up, dusting yourself off, and starting over looks like.

She taught me that although life doesn't always turn out the way you planned, there are still beautiful moments to be had every single day. She also taught me that it is never too late to accomplish your dreams. She didn't always understand why I wanted to start a podcast or become an energy healer, but she was my biggest cheerleader. In fact, if you look up my first book on Amazon, she was the first one to leave a review. I thought that was very touching, and it also makes me laugh that my mom was my first reviewer. Of course, she was. She made me realize that everyone needs that cheerleader in life. I was lucky to have had a mom who was such a shining example of a fearless, badass, strong woman.

I consider myself blessed to have had two parents who weren't afraid of change and who modeled that for us. They both taught me that pursuing your passion will always pay off in the end. My dad also went back to school later in life to pursue a new career in nursing. That is never an easy thing to do. It takes strength and fortitude to leave what is comfortable in order to live out your passion. It isn't too late for you to do the same thing. What are you passionate about? What have you always wanted to do but never done? I heard someone say one time after their loved one died that they were just waiting to die. That statement was incredibly sad to me, but I understood what that person meant. The person meant that they were just going through the motions in life. Without their loved one, they didn't really feel like there was anything exciting worth living for. While I do empathize with that, I also want to encourage anyone who feels this way to change their mindset. Remember, if you don't like how things are, change them. Now is the perfect time to start exploring all the different avenues of life that are available to you. Remember, you are rebranding yourself.

It's true that I am not the same since my mom's death. Grief changed me in so many ways and taught me so many unexpected lessons. It made me realize that just because life didn't turn out the way I thought it would, that doesn't mean that life isn't still worth living. I've had to learn to be flexible in my thinking and more patient with myself and others. I learned that grief takes time, and it comes in waves. Not everyone will grieve the same way, and not everyone will understand your grief. Give yourself and others grace. Another important thing that I learned is that my mom would have wanted me to move on and be happy, and your loved one wants you to move on and be happy too. The good news is that it is totally possible.

On this journey, I have had to redefine many of the relationships in my life. I had to learn to allow others to support me emotionally, which does not come naturally to me. I watched some of my friends and family band together to support one another, while watching other friends and family members drift away. I have had people that I thought would be there no matter what drop out of my life.

That was really painful. I have had to learn to let go of people and things who weren't serving my highest good, which was a tough lesson for me. I learned to give people only what they give you. If there are people in your life who do not put in the same effort that you do, then let those people go. Life is too short to over-give in relationships. I learned that grief affects everyone differently and not everyone will grieve in a healthy way, but I can only control myself and the way I grieve. I had to learn to set boundaries for myself and start trusting myself more. I had to learn how to love and connect to my mom in a new way. Yes, I have to live without her physical presence, but I can hold onto the love that she left behind. I discovered how to ask for help when I needed it, especially from professionals. Life is not the same, and it will never be the same again; now I am making adjustments to my life to accommodate that change.

Grief changes us. We can allow it to make us bitter, or we can allow it to make us better. It's our choice. I choose to see how it changed me for the better. It helped me grow exponentially as a person. I'm more empathetic, patient, and I value things that are truly important in life. I could dwell on everything that I lost when my mom's soul left this Earth, or I can focus on everything she gave me while she was here. I choose to focus on the latter. I choose to rely on the strength that she showed me through the example that she was as a mom. If you are struggling to move forward and are stuck in your grief right now, I understand. It is a very difficult thing to comprehend why our loved ones have to leave us, and it leaves a huge hole in our hearts and lives. As Elizabeth Kubler Ross said, "The reality is that you will grieve forever. You will not 'get over' the loss of a loved one; you will learn to live with it. You will heal, and you will rebuild yourself around the loss that you have suffered. You will be whole again, but you will never be the same. Nor should you be the same, nor would you want to be." Her words are so important because if we are here to learn, then grief should change us. That change doesn't have to be a negative thing. You will rebuild, you will move on, and it is my hope that the tools I have given you, as well as other outside assistance, will help you get through this a little easier.

First of all, I want you to understand that life will go on, and it will get a little easier with each and every passing day. I agree with Elizabeth Kubler Ross in that I don't know that the pain of loss ever truly leaves us, but it does become more manageable. Here are some things that I want you to do if you are still having a difficult time moving forward. The very first thing I want you to do is to stop placing unrealistic expectations on yourself. Believing that you should magically feel better by a certain time is impractical. Grief doesn't have an expiration date. Be patient with yourself when you have a bad day, a bad week, or even a bad month. That is going to happen from time to time. Also, it's perfectly normal to feel better one day and sad again the next.

As I said before, grief comes in waves. It's like the ebb and flow of the tides. It is ever present. You know that it is always there. One moment it is washing over you, and you feel as though you are drowning. The next moment, it eases up and is no longer engulfing you. It just barely grazes your feet as you are walking along the shore of life. Just this past weekend, I had two days when I felt weepy all day. I cried off and on. I haven't felt like that in a long time. It just hits you without warning from time to time. Sometimes there is a trigger that sets it off, and sometimes it just shows up out of the blue. Be patient with yourself. The next thing I want you to do is to gather a list of tools that you can have at your disposal when you have a bad day. These tools can help you to move through your grief more easily. It is important to honor how you are feeling, but you don't have to wallow in it.

I am going to give you some tips and tools that I have used in my own life to help me work through grief with grace. The first tip is to rely on your tribe. I recommend that you have a support group to reach out to. Whether you go to individual counseling or a grief group, or if you have a group of friends that you can rely on, you need to have people to talk to. Talking through your feelings will help. Remember that if you bottle your emotions up, you will get sick. Those emotions don't just disappear. They get trapped in your body. Rely on your support group and don't hesitate to ask for help. Most of us do not want to admit when we are struggling, but that is the whole purpose of having a support system. They are there to help you. Please ask for help when you need it.

The next thing I suggest is having a list of activities that make you feel better. Maybe you enjoy baking or going for walks, or perhaps you love reading a good book; whatever you enjoy doing most is what is important. I want you to make a list of all the activities that you enjoy. When you have a bad day, I want you to pull out that list of activities and pick one to do. You could even make a game out of it by closing your eyes and randomly picking something. I also understand that when those moments of grief hit you, they can be so intense that you don't feel like doing anything. If you have a day where you need a time out, take it. If you'd like to feel better, and I know you do, then make yourself go do something. It may suck just a little at first, but you will be glad you did. It helps to distract our brains sometimes. The goal is to get yourself back out there enjoying life again. Don't isolate yourself. When people invite you to go places, go with them. It will do you good to be around others.

When you are feeling emotional, have a good cry. It's healthy to do that. Then I want you to think of some memories that make you laugh. I want you to think of everything that you loved about the person you lost. If you are a creative person, perhaps you could make something in memory of your loved one. I am writing this book in honor of my mom. It is helping me to move through my grief tremendously. Maybe you write poetry or songs, or you might be an artist who likes to paint. Use your talents to honor your loved one. Someone made us pillows out of my mom's shirts. It was such a thoughtful gesture, and now I have something that feels like a little piece of her with me. Maybe you can make something meaningful out of your loved one's old things too. I think creating and art are great ways to work through painful emotions. There is a reason that they use art therapy with children. Art allows us to express what we are feeling in a safe and beautiful way.

Another important way to move through your grief is to practice self-care. So many people let this go when they are grieving. I've seen people develop terrible habits that are harmful to the body because they don't care if they live or die. Your loved one does not want you to do that to yourself. They would want you to take good care of yourself. Make sure that you are getting enough rest, stay hydrated, and move your body a little every day. I always used to joke with my podcast audience that I hated yoga. I really thought I did. I could never get into it. After my mom died, I tried a quick 15-minute yoga routine, and I was amazed at how much it helped me. I felt more calm and relaxed, and as an added bonus, I slept much better at night. I had a really hard time sleeping after my mom first passed. I believe that yoga helped me to release stress, which in turn lowered my cortisol levels, which helped me to sleep deeper and longer through the night. It was a win-win for me. If you don't like yoga, you can try other forms of movement. Try learning a new dance or do some strength training. Even just going for a quick walk can help. Movement is so important. It helps stabilize our mood, and it helps us to balance emotions and our hormones.

One of the things I love doing the most is writing. I know that not everyone enjoys it, but writing is such a powerful tool. I think that journaling is a fantastic way to work through what it is we are feeling, and we can use it to create goals for ourselves, shift our mindsets, and it can help us heal. Here are a few journal prompts that you can use to help support you in moving through your grief. Find some time and a quiet place to sit and write. Pick one or two prompts to answer each day.

- What am I feeling today?

- What is one thing I want to remember about my loved one?

- Today I miss...

- I need more of...in my life

- I need less of...in my life

- Do I need help with anything in my life right now? Am I comfortable asking for help? Why or why not?

- One thing I wish I could do differently is...

- I connect most closely to my loved one through...

- What is one mantra I can use when I feel overwhelmed by grief?

- Is there anyone else going through grief right now? How can I support them?

- What is something that I wish everyone would understand about grief?

- If you could tell your loved one something about your life right now, what would you say?

- If I could forgive myself for one thing right now…what would that be?

- What is one thing that I have always wanted to try?

- What is one thing that I loved most about my loved one?

- If I had the courage to change one thing in my life right now, what would it be?

- What songs make me think of my loved one?

- What is something I need my support group to help me with?

- What is one thing I want to tell my loved one?

- What makes me truly happy?

Using these journaling prompts can help you to work through the tough emotions that are brought on by grief, and they can help you to work on creating a life you love. You will discover what is no longer serving you in life so that you can release it. You will also learn what makes you happy and brings you joy so that you can start doing more of those things in your everyday life. Maybe you had a difficult relationship with your loved one. Journaling can help you do some much-needed forgiveness work too.

Whether you need to forgive yourself or your loved one or both, forgiveness is so freeing. You will feel so much better once you let go of the guilt, shame, anger, resentment, and any other negative emotion that is related to forgiveness.

Another great tool to have in your arsenal is meditation. There are some amazing and free guided meditations on YouTube. I have one that I created on my YouTube channel that walks you through talking to someone's higher self in order to achieve forgiveness. Meditation is also a great way to relax your mind. Plus, there are meditations that can help you connect with your loved one too. I have seen many guided meditations that allow you to connect to your guides or to crossed-over loved ones. Meditation is amazing for your mental and emotional health. It has wonderful physiological effects on the body like lowering blood pressure and stress levels. It can also help you sleep better at night if you do one before bedtime. If I am feeling out of sorts or in a funk, I do a short meditation. It can shift your mood in a quick and easy way. Meditation is also a great way to help release some of those tough negative emotions that come up with grief.

I've talked about Tapping before, but I think it is such a wonderful tool. EFT, or Emotional Freedom Technique, allows you to unlock the deep emotions that you store in your body. Once we unlock them, we can release them, and then we can begin shifting our perception of reality. Instead of feeling bad, we can actually start to feel good.

One thing that I would like to say is that you have to find what works for you. I am giving you a list of tools that I use, but you may find that some do not work for you, or you may not enjoy using a particular tool. That is perfectly fine. You have to find things that work for you. I used to joke that I hated doing yoga. I wished that I liked it because everyone raved about it. After my mom died, something changed in me. I decided to give yoga one more try, and this time I loved it. I was used to working out with high intensity cardio or strength training. Those became too much for me when I was first grieving. I just didn't have the energy or stamina to keep up, nor did I want to even try. I found a quick yoga routine and decided to try it. I really enjoyed it, and that night I was so relaxed. I really feel like it helped me to connect to my body and how I was feeling so that I could process it easier. That is super important when you are grieving because sometimes we are all over the place. Our emotions can run amok. My point is that you have to be willing to try things. If they work, great. If they don't, go try something else. You will eventually find something that helps you.

Energy healing is also a very effective tool in working through grief and trauma. Reiki, biofield tuning, and other energetic healing modalities are wonderful. They allow you to release the emotional pain that the body is holding without having to walk back through the trauma that caused it. It's also very relaxing and a great way to release tension and stress. Remember how important it is to release old emotions. They stay stored in our body when we don't process them. That causes physical illness in the body. You don't have to have had a lot of trauma in your life to have stored up emotions. I do believe that we are all exposed to trauma in life. I always say that just being born was traumatic. Honestly, living through Covid was enough trauma for most people to last a lifetime. It's critical to release your emotions from time to time. Think of your body like an etch-a-sketch. You can't keep drawing on it once the screen is full. You have to shake it to clear out the old drawings. Then you can start over and create new things. It's the same with your body. You have to clear the old negative junk, so you can fill up your body with beautiful healed energy.

Whether it takes you six months, a year, 20 years or more, you will begin to heal from your grief. Slowly and with passing time, your pain becomes a little less intense. You start to breathe a little easier. I'm not saying that you will never grieve again for your loved one once you start to heal. Grief is like the moon. Even though we don't usually see it during the day, it never really goes away. We always know it's there. Some nights it is full and shines so brightly you will be overcome by its power. Other nights, you don't see it at all because it's covered by a cloudy sky. You still know it's there, but it doesn't have that powerful effect on you. In the same way, some days grief may hold you in its tight grip, while other days you have so many other beautiful things going on that you don't even realize it's there.

Little by little, your life will go back to a state of normalcy. Have patience with yourself and the process. Remember to take breaks when you need them and rely on a support system. Practice self-care every day. Continue to have faith that things will get easier for you. I saw this quote by John Green that I think makes a wonderful point: "So often we try to make other people feel better by minimizing their pain, by telling them that it will get better (which it will) or that there are worse things in the world (which there are). But that's not what I actually needed. What I needed was for someone to tell me that it hurt because it mattered." You don't have to try and minimize your pain. It does hurt, and it does matter. Acknowledge it and allow it to be a part of you, but you also don't have to allow it to consume you. Your pain is real, and your grief is real because the love you had was real as well. I think Elan Mastai sums it up perfectly in this quote: "People talk about grief as emptiness, but it's not empty. It's full. Heavy. Not an absence to fill. A weight to pull. Your skin caught on hooks chained to rough boulders made of all the futures you thought you'd have." What imagery that inspires. It reminds me of the movie Saw. She is correct, though. Grief is tough. It's heavy. It's downright brutal. It's an extremely tricky path to navigate. You will have good days, and you will have bad days. Remember that on your worst days if all you do is breathe, that's ok too. There are still better days coming. There are still wonderful experiences to be had, and I believe that eventually we will see our loved ones again. I take a great deal of comfort in that.

Grief has changed the person that I am, but here I am. I am still living. Grief can either destroy you or transform you. You can choose to put up armor around your heart and never let someone in again because you could lose them too, or you can shift your perspective to see what an enormous blessing it is to share so much love with another human being. That connection we create is unique and beautiful. It is always worth the energy and effort to create such heartfelt connections with others, even if we lose them in the end. After all, life has to end, but love does not. It's true that we never truly get over a loss, but we can grow from it. Death can be our greatest teacher if we let it. You can try to escape the lessons that it teaches, but in the end, you came here to learn. You have to learn, whether you want to or not. Love and death are our greatest gifts. Death leaves many lessons. May we learn that time is not to be wasted. That love is not to be taken for granted. That moments are to be cherished. And that love is real and eternal. My hope and prayer for each and every one of you is that you continue to live your life, not just surviving…but thriving. You deserve to feel joy and peace again. There are so many amazing adventures waiting for you.

Life is short, and you know that better than anyone. Don't sit and let life pass you by. Take chances and risks, love fiercely, be good to yourself, and most importantly, I hope you dance.

A Mother's Love

A mother's love is a fearsome thing to behold. Nothing compares to its beauty. A mother loves you, protects you, prays for you, cries with you, and yes, loses sleep over you. Mothers aren't perfect, but their love transcends perfection. They may not always know the right way to react to situations, but one thing is for certain, you know their love for you runs deep. The most incredible thing about this love is that there is nothing you have to do to earn it. It was created the moment your life existed and possibly even before.

A mother-child relationship can be a very complicated thing. Adolescence is often confusing and messy. It often creates a strife between mother and child. I know there were times when I disappointed my mom as I was finding my way in life, but I knew no matter what I said or did, she'd never stop loving me. Yes, we quarreled. Yes, I hurt her, and yes, she wished for better things for me. One thing I knew to be true is that no matter what, she was always there for me. No matter how many times I broke her heart, she never closed it off to me. I had her whole heart, and I knew it. She knew it too. A love like that is rare. Not everyone is privileged to experience it, but I was.

This love is something I leaned on for over forty years. I assumed I would always have it. It's only now that I have really learned to appreciate it. After becoming a mom myself, I understand the immense joy and responsibility that motherhood brings. There is an incredible void in my heart and in my life not having that unconditional love. I miss so many things about my mom. In my head I know that her love never truly dies if her memory still lives within us, but I can't seem to make my heart understand. I miss her laugh, her hugs, and all of the things that made her uniquely her. Most of all, I miss her presence. She was such a big energy, and she knew how to fill a room with it. There are days when I can still hear her voice. She says to me, "Every little thing is going to be alright." There are days when I can still feel her hugs. Then there are days when she feels light years away. A mother isn't perfect, but her love is. It's what you need when someone breaks your heart. It's what you crave when you want to celebrate good news. It's what you grieve when it's no longer there. A mother's love is a complicated, yet beautiful thing. Here's to my mother, the strongest woman I knew. Here's to all the strong women and mothers out there. May we know them. May we be them. May we raise them.

I love you, Mama.

www.ingramcontent.com/pod-product-compliance
Lightning Source LLC
Chambersburg PA
CBHW051150120626
46547CB00012B/1021